Data Science Fusion: Integrating Maths, Python, and Machine Learning

Published by Nibedita Sahu

Data Science Fusion: Integrating Maths, Python, and Machine Learning

Written by Nibedita Sahu

Table of Contents

Data Science Fusion: Integrating Maths, Python, and Machine Learning 1
Chapter 1: Understanding Data Science 9
Chapter 2: The Data Science Workflow 10
Chapter 3: Tools and Technologies in Data Science 11
Chapter 4: Foundations of Mathematics for Data Science 12
Chapter 5: Linear Algebra for Data Scientists 13
Chapter 6: Multivariable Calculus: A Data Science Perspective 14
Chapter 7: Probability and Statistics for Data Analysis 15
Chapter 8: Python Fundamentals 16
Chapter 9: Essential Python Libraries for Data Science 17
Chapter 10: Data Wrangling and Preprocessing with Python 18
Chapter 11: Data Visualization Techniques with Matplotlib and Seaborn 19

Chapter 12: Introduction to Machine Learning 20
Chapter 13: Supervised Learning: Regression and Classification 21
Chapter 14: Unsupervised Learning: Clustering and Dimensionality Reduction 22
Chapter 15: Evaluation Metrics for Machine Learning Models 23
Chapter 16: Ensembles and Boosting Algorithms 24
Chapter 17: Deep Learning Fundamentals 25
Chapter 18: Convolutional Neural Networks (CNNs) for Image Analysis 26
Chapter 19: Recurrent Neural Networks (RNNs) for Sequence Data 27
Chapter 20: Natural Language Processing (NLP) with Machine Learning 28
Chapter 1: Understanding Data Science 40
Chapter 2: The Data Science Workflow 60
Chapter 3: Tools and Technologies in Data Science 94

Chapter 4: Foundations of Mathematics for Data Science 127
Chapter 5: Linear Algebra for Data Scientists 153
Chapter 6: Multivariable Calculus: A Data Science Perspective 184
Chapter 7: Probability and Statistics for Data Analysis 206
Chapter 8: Python Fundamentals 228
Chapter 9: Essential Python Libraries for Data Science 263
Chapter 10: Data Wrangling and Preprocessing with Python 279
Chapter 11: Data Visualization Techniques with Matplotlib and Seaborn 299
Chapter 12: Introduction to Machine Learning 323
Chapter 13: Supervised Learning: Regression and Classification 343
Chapter 14: Unsupervised Learning: Clustering and Dimensionality Reduction 363
Chapter 15: Evaluation Metrics for Machine Learning Models 386

Chapter 16: Ensembles and Boosting Algorithms...412
Chapter 17: Deep Learning Fundamentals... 441
Chapter 18: Convolutional Neural Networks (CNNs) for Image Analysis 470
Chapter 19: Recurrent Neural Networks (RNNs) for Sequence Data....................................503
Chapter 20: Natural Language Processing (NLP) with Machine Learning............................. 537

Preface:

Welcome to "Data Science Fusion: Integrating Maths, Python, and Machine Learning"! In this book, we embark on an exciting journey through the realms of data science, machine learning, mathematics, and Python programming. The mission is to equip you with the knowledge and skills to harness the power of data and turn it into valuable insights.

The field of data science has emerged as a cornerstone of the digital age, revolutionizing industries and transforming the way we approach problem-solving. With the explosion of data, there is an ever-increasing demand for skilled data scientists who can not only understand the data but also interpret it effectively. This book is designed to meet this demand by providing a comprehensive and cohesive resource that brings together the key pillars of data science.

Whether you are a complete beginner, an intermediate learner, or an advanced practitioner, this book caters to your needs. Intermediate learners will find this book to be a stepping stone in their data science journey. Fear not if you find mathematics intimidating; the author provided intuitive explanations and practical applications of these mathematical concepts in data science. For advanced practitioners, this book is an opportunity to explore cutting-edge machine learning techniques, deep dive into advanced Python libraries, and uncover the secrets of model performance optimization. The integration of mathematics with machine learning is a key theme throughout the book, showing how mathematics is not just theory but a powerful tool in the hands of data scientists.

As you progress through "Data Science Fusion," you'll witness the fusion of mathematics, Python programming, and machine learning, resulting in a synergistic approach to data science.

Hope this book not only imparts valuable knowledge but also sparks a passion for data science and the possibilities it holds. Whether your journey is just beginning or you are a seasoned data practitioner,

let's dive in and unlock the potential of data together!

Objectives and Goals:

The main objectives of "Data Science Fusion" are to empower individuals with a comprehensive understanding of data science, machine learning, and their integration with mathematics using Python. The book aims to achieve the following goals:

1. Provide a Solid Foundation in Data Science: The book starts by introducing the fundamental concepts of data science, covering the entire data science workflow from data collection to insights generation. It aims to give readers a holistic understanding of the data science process and its significance in various industries.

2. Integrate Mathematics with Data Science: One of the primary goals of this book is to demystify the mathematical concepts essential for data science. By explaining linear algebra, calculus, probability, and statistics in a data science context, the book ensures that readers can seamlessly apply mathematical insights to solve data-related problems.

3. Master Python for Data Science: The book extensively covers Python programming, providing readers with a strong foundation in Python's data manipulation, visualization, and analysis libraries (NumPy, Pandas, Matplotlib). With practical examples and hands-on projects, the book aims to equip readers with the necessary Python skills for data science.

4. Explore the Landscape of Machine Learning: "Data Science Fusion" delves into the world of machine learning, offering a detailed overview of supervised and unsupervised learning techniques. It covers essential algorithms, evaluation metrics, and best practices, ensuring readers gain a well-rounded understanding of machine learning fundamentals.

5. Showcase Advanced Machine Learning Techniques: Beyond the basics, the book dives into advanced machine learning approaches, including ensembles, deep learning, and natural language processing. The goal is to provide readers with exposure to state-of-the-art techniques and an opportunity to tackle complex data science challenges.

6. Emphasize Integration and Application: Throughout the book, the integration of mathematical concepts into Python-based data science projects takes center stage. Practical projects, case studies, and real-world examples demonstrate how to implement data science solutions effectively.

7. Cater to Diverse Audiences: While the book is designed for beginners, intermediate learners, and advanced practitioners, the goal is to strike a balance between accessibility and depth. By tailoring the content and language, the book aims to cater to the varying backgrounds and expertise levels of its readers.

8. Foster Ethical and Responsible Data Science: The book emphasizes ethical considerations in data science and machine learning, promoting responsible practices and raising awareness of potential biases and ethical challenges in data-driven decision-making.

In conclusion, "Data Science Fusion: Integrating Maths, Python, and Machine Learning" aspires to equip readers with the essential knowledge, skills, and practical insights required to excel in the dynamic and ever-evolving field of data science. By integrating mathematics, Python, and machine learning, the book aims to empower readers to harness the power of data and make informed, data-driven decisions in various domains.

Book Outline: Data Science Fusion: Integrating Maths, Python, and Machine Learning

Unit I: Introduction to Data Science

Chapter 1: Understanding Data Science

1.1. Definition of Data Science

1.2. Importance and Applications of Data Science

1.3. Data Science in Various Industries

Chapter 2: The Data Science Workflow

2.1. Data Collection and Data Sources

2.2. Data Cleaning and Preprocessing

2.3. Exploratory Data Analysis (EDA)

2.4. Feature Engineering

Chapter 3: Tools and Technologies in Data Science

3.1. Introduction to Python for Data Science

3.2. Key Python Libraries: NumPy, Pandas, and Matplotlib

3.3. Virtual Environments for Data Science Projects

Unit II: The Mathematics of Data Science

Chapter 4: Foundations of Mathematics for Data Science

4.1. Number Systems and Arithmetic Operations

4.2. Sets, Relations, and Functions

4.3. Logic and Propositional Calculus

Chapter 5: Linear Algebra for Data Scientists

5.1. Vectors and Matrices

5.2. Matrix Operations: Addition, Multiplication, and Inverse

5.3. Eigenvalues and Eigenvectors

Chapter 6: Multivariable Calculus: A Data Science Perspective

6.1. Partial Derivatives and Gradients

6.2. Optimization: Minimization and Maximization

6.3. Applications of Multivariable Calculus in Data Science

Chapter 7: Probability and Statistics for Data Analysis

7.1. Probability Distributions: Discrete and Continuous

7.2. Statistical Measures: Mean, Median, Variance, and Standard Deviation

7.3. Hypothesis Testing and Confidence Intervals

Unit III: Python for Data Science

Chapter 8: Python Fundamentals

8.1. Variables and Data Types

8.2. Control Flow: Loops and Conditionals

8.3. Functions and Object-Oriented Programming in Python

Chapter 9: Essential Python Libraries for Data Science

9.1. NumPy for Numerical Computing

9.2. Pandas for Data Manipulation and Analysis

9.3. Matplotlib for Data Visualization

Chapter 10: Data Wrangling and Preprocessing with Python

10.1. Data Cleaning Techniques

10.2. Data Transformation and Feature Scaling

10.3. Handling Missing Data

Chapter 11: Data Visualization Techniques with Matplotlib and Seaborn

11.1. Creating Basic Plots: Line, Bar, and Scatter

11.2. Customizing Plots for Effective Visualization

11.3. Advanced Visualization: Heatmaps, Subplots, and 3D Plots

Unit IV: Machine Learning Basics

Chapter 12: Introduction to Machine Learning

12.1. Supervised, Unsupervised, and Reinforcement Learning

12.2. Overfitting, Underfitting, and Bias-Variance Tradeoff

12.3. Cross-Validation and Model Selection

Chapter 13: Supervised Learning: Regression and Classification

13.1. Linear Regression and Polynomial Regression

13.2. Logistic Regression for Binary and Multiclass Classification

13.3. Decision Trees and Random Forests

Chapter 14: Unsupervised Learning: Clustering and Dimensionality Reduction

14.1. K-Means Clustering

14.2. Hierarchical Clustering

14.3. Principal Component Analysis (PCA) for Dimensionality Reduction

Chapter 15: Evaluation Metrics for Machine Learning Models

15.1. Accuracy, Precision, Recall, and F1 Score

15.2. Confusion Matrix and ROC Curve

15.3. Regression Metrics: MSE, MAE, and R-squared

Unit V: Advanced Machine Learning Techniques

Chapter 16: Ensembles and Boosting Algorithms

16.1. Bagging and Boosting Concepts

16.2. Random Forests and Gradient Boosting

16.3. XGBoost and LightGBM

Chapter 17: Deep Learning Fundamentals

17.1. Neural Networks: Architecture and Layers

17.2. Activation Functions and Backpropagation

17.3. Loss Functions for Neural Networks

Chapter 18: Convolutional Neural Networks (CNNs) for Image Analysis

18.1. Understanding CNN Architecture

18.2. Image Recognition and Classification with CNNs

18.3. Transfer Learning and Fine-Tuning

Chapter 19: Recurrent Neural Networks (RNNs) for Sequence Data

19.1. Introduction to RNNs and LSTM

19.2. Text Generation with RNNs

19.3. Sequence-to-Sequence Models for Language Translation

Chapter 20: Natural Language Processing (NLP) with Machine Learning

20.1. Text Preprocessing and Tokenization

20.2. Word Embeddings: Word2Vec and GloVe

20.3. Sentiment Analysis and Text Classification with NLP

Target Audience:

This book is designed to cater to a broad range of individuals interested in data science, machine learning, and their integration with mathematics using Python. The target audience is segmented into three main categories:

Beginners: This book is suitable for individuals with little to no prior experience in data science, machine learning, or programming. Beginners who are eager to embark on a journey into the world of data science and want to understand how mathematics, Python, and machine learning intersect will find this book to be an excellent starting point.

Intermediate Learners: Intermediate learners who already possess a foundational understanding of data science concepts and programming in Python will benefit from this book's comprehensive coverage of mathematics and advanced machine learning techniques. This segment includes readers who want to deepen their knowledge and gain proficiency in integrating mathematical concepts into data science workflows using Python.

Advanced Practitioners: Even seasoned data scientists and machine learning practitioners can find value in this book. Advanced practitioners will appreciate the book's focus on the integration of mathematical insights into Python-based data science projects, as well as the detailed exploration of cutting-edge machine learning algorithms and practices.

Summary: Data Science Fusion: Integrating Maths, Python, and Machine Learning

"Data Science Fusion: Integrating Maths, Python, and Machine Learning" is a comprehensive and accessible guide that empowers readers to navigate the multifaceted world of data science with confidence. The book is meticulously crafted to cater to beginners, intermediate learners, and advanced practitioners, offering a seamless fusion of mathematics, Python programming, and machine learning concepts.

The journey begins with an introduction to data science, unveiling its significance, applications, and the key stages of the data science workflow. Readers are then equipped with the essential mathematical foundations for data science, including linear algebra, multivariable calculus, probability, and statistics. These mathematical insights serve as the bedrock for the subsequent integration of data science with Python.

Python, the cornerstone of modern data science, is thoroughly explored in the book, covering core concepts, essential libraries (NumPy, Pandas, Matplotlib), and data wrangling techniques. The integration of mathematics and Python becomes the driving force behind data science projects, enabling readers to seamlessly apply mathematical concepts to real-world datasets. The book delves into the vast realm of machine learning, starting with supervised and unsupervised learning techniques. Fundamental algorithms and evaluation metrics are elucidated to provide a comprehensive understanding of model performance and selection.

In its pursuit of holistic learning, the book takes a step further by immersing readers in advanced machine learning techniques, including ensembles, deep learning with neural networks, and natural language processing. The practical projects and case studies presented throughout the book provide readers with invaluable experience in applying machine learning to solve diverse data science challenges.

The integration theme persists as the book introduces mathematical insights into machine learning algorithms, illustrating the powerful synergy between mathematics and Python programming. Throughout the journey, ethical considerations in data science are emphasized, cultivating a sense of responsibility and awareness in data-driven decision-making.

In conclusion, "Data Science Fusion" is a tour de force that equips readers with the essential knowledge and practical skills required to embark on a successful data science journey. It seamlessly bridges the gap between mathematical theory and Python programming, enabling readers to leverage the full potential of data science and machine learning in diverse domains. Whether starting from scratch or seeking to enhance existing expertise, this book is a valuable resource for anyone seeking to unlock the power of data science fusion.

Unit I: Introduction to Data Science

Data science is a multidisciplinary field that encompasses a diverse range of techniques, processes, and methodologies used to extract knowledge and insights from data. It combines elements of mathematics, statistics, computer science, domain expertise, and domain-specific knowledge to make informed decisions and predictions. In the modern age, where data has become a powerful resource, data science plays a pivotal role in transforming raw data into meaningful and actionable information.

At its core, data science revolves around the concept of harnessing data to gain valuable insights and drive better decision-making. With the proliferation of technology and the internet, vast amounts of data are generated every day. This data comes from various sources such as social media interactions, online purchases, sensors, medical records, and more. However, raw data alone is of limited use; the real value lies in understanding and extracting patterns and trends hidden within this vast sea of information.

The data science workflow typically involves several key stages:

>>> Data Collection: The first step is to gather data from diverse sources relevant to the problem at hand. This data can be structured (like databases) or unstructured (like text or images).

>>> Data Cleaning and Preprocessing: Often, data may contain errors, missing values, or inconsistencies. Data scientists need to clean and preprocess the data to ensure its quality and prepare it for analysis.

>>> Data Exploration and Visualization: In this stage, data scientists explore the data to uncover meaningful patterns, trends, and correlations. Visualization techniques are used to represent the data graphically, making it easier to understand and interpret.

>>> Data Modeling: In this crucial phase, data scientists apply various mathematical and statistical techniques to build predictive models. These models can help in making predictions or classifications based on new data.

>>> Model Training and Evaluation: The models are trained using historical data, and their performance is evaluated using metrics like accuracy, precision, recall, etc. This step helps in identifying the best-performing model for the specific problem.

>>> Deployment and Monitoring: Once a model is selected, it is deployed in real-world scenarios to make predictions or support decision-making. Continuous monitoring ensures the model's performance remains optimal over time.

Data science finds applications in a wide range of fields, including business, healthcare, finance, marketing, social sciences, and more. In business, data science is instrumental in optimizing operations, understanding customer behaviour, and making data-driven business strategies. In healthcare, it aids in disease prediction, diagnosis, and drug discovery. In finance, data science is used for fraud detection, risk assessment, and algorithmic trading.

Machine learning, a subfield of data science, plays a crucial role in automating the extraction of knowledge from data. It involves the use of algorithms that learn from data to improve their performance on a specific task. Supervised learning, unsupervised learning, and reinforcement learning are common paradigms within machine learning.

Supervised learning involves training a model using labeled data, where the model learns to map inputs to corresponding outputs. Unsupervised learning, on the other hand, deals with unlabeled data and aims to find patterns and structures within the data. Reinforcement learning focuses on an agent learning to make decisions by interacting with an environment and receiving feedback in the form of rewards.

Data science is a rapidly evolving and influential field that empowers individuals and organizations to make better decisions and solve complex problems. As the world becomes increasingly data-driven, the demand for skilled data scientists continues to grow. Understanding the principles and methodologies of data science opens up a world of opportunities to explore, analyze, and leverage the power of data for the betterment of society and various industries.

Chapter 1: Understanding Data Science

1. Definition of Data Science

Data Science is a multidisciplinary field that combines techniques, processes, and methodologies from various domains to extract knowledge, insights, and meaningful patterns from raw data. It involves a systematic approach to understanding data, using mathematical and statistical tools, and leveraging advanced technologies to make data-driven decisions and predictions. Data science has gained immense popularity and importance in recent years due to the explosion of data and the growing need to extract valuable information from it.

At the core of data science lies data, which can be generated from a plethora of sources, such as social media interactions, online transactions, scientific experiments, sensors, and more. This data can be structured, like databases, or unstructured, such as text, images, audio, and video. The massive volume, velocity, and variety of data, known as the three V's of big data, pose both challenges and opportunities for data scientists.

The data science process typically begins with data collection, where data from diverse sources is gathered and stored for analysis. However, before delving into data analysis, it is essential to ensure data quality. Data cleaning and preprocessing involve dealing with missing values, eliminating errors, handling outliers, and transforming data into a suitable format. This step is crucial, as the accuracy and reliability of the insights derived from data are highly dependent on the quality of the data used.

Once the data is pre-processed, the next stage is data exploration and visualization. Data scientists employ various statistical and visualization techniques to gain a deeper understanding of the data. Exploratory Data Analysis (EDA) helps identify patterns, trends, correlations, and outliers that may not be apparent at first glance. Visualization aids in representing the data graphically, making it easier to communicate insights to stakeholders.

The heart of data science lies in data modeling. This involves the application of mathematical and statistical algorithms to build predictive models from the data. Supervised learning is a common approach where the model is trained using labeled data, where the input and output relationships are known. The goal is to learn from the training data and predict the output for new, unseen data.

On the other hand, unsupervised learning deals with unlabeled data and aims to find patterns and structures within the data without explicit guidance. Clustering, dimensionality reduction, and association rule mining are some of the techniques used in unsupervised learning.

Another important aspect of data science is reinforcement learning, where an agent learns to make decisions by interacting with an environment and receiving feedback in the form of rewards or penalties. Reinforcement learning has applications in areas like robotics, game playing, and autonomous systems.

Once the models are trained, they need to be evaluated for their performance. Various metrics, such as accuracy, precision, recall, F1 score, and ROC-AUC, are used to assess how well the model performs on unseen data. Model evaluation helps in identifying the best-performing model for a given task.

The deployment and monitoring of the model in real-world scenarios is the next step. The model is integrated into the operational systems to make predictions or support decision-making. Continuous monitoring of the model's performance ensures that it remains effective over time, and any drift in data distribution is detected early.

Data science has found applications across numerous domains. In the business world, data science plays a vital role in customer segmentation, recommendation systems, fraud detection, and demand forecasting. In healthcare, data science aids in medical imaging analysis, disease prediction, personalized treatment plans, and drug discovery.

Social sciences utilize data science for sentiment analysis, social network analysis, and understanding human behaviour. Governments and public policy makers use data science to gain insights into citizen needs, optimize public services, and improve governance.

Ethics and privacy are crucial considerations in data science. As data scientists work with sensitive and personal data, ensuring data privacy, security, and responsible use of data is of utmost importance. Data anonymization, secure data storage, and compliance with data protection regulations are essential aspects of ethical data science practices.

In conclusion, data science is a dynamic and transformative field that empowers individuals, organizations, and societies to leverage the power of data for better decision-making and problem-solving. The continuous evolution of data science techniques and the integration of artificial intelligence and machine learning have opened up new possibilities and opportunities in various sectors. By harnessing the potential of data, data science plays a pivotal role in shaping a data-driven future.

1. Importance and Applications of Data Science

Data science has emerged as a critical discipline in the modern world due to the explosive growth of data and the need to extract valuable insights from it. The abundance of data generated from various sources, such as social media, sensors, online transactions, and scientific research, presents both challenges and opportunities. Data science plays a pivotal role in converting raw data into actionable information, facilitating data-driven decision-making, and driving innovation across a wide range of industries and domains.

Importance of Data Science:

>>> Data-Driven Decision Making: In today's data-centric world, making decisions based on intuition or guesswork is no longer sufficient. Data science enables organizations to make informed decisions by analyzing historical and real-time data, identifying trends, and predicting future outcomes. Data-driven decision-making leads to better resource allocation, improved efficiency, and higher success rates.

>>> Business Intelligence and Analytics: Data science is a cornerstone of business intelligence and analytics. It helps organizations gain insights into customer behavior, market trends, and competitor analysis. This information aids in formulating effective marketing strategies, optimizing product offerings, and staying ahead in the competitive landscape.

>>> Personalization and Customer Experience: Data science allows companies to personalize products and services based on individual preferences and behavior patterns. Recommendation systems, powered by data science, offer personalized suggestions to customers, enhancing their overall experience and increasing customer satisfaction.

>>> Predictive Maintenance: In industries like manufacturing, aviation, and energy, data science enables predictive maintenance. By analyzing sensor data and historical performance, data scientists can predict equipment failures and schedule maintenance proactively, reducing downtime and saving costs.

>>> Healthcare and Medicine: Data science is revolutionizing healthcare by enabling precision medicine, disease prediction, and personalized treatment plans.

Analyzing medical records, genomic data, and patient history helps identify genetic predispositions to diseases, optimize treatment options, and improve patient outcomes.

>>> ***Fraud Detection and Security:*** Data science plays a crucial role in fraud detection and cybersecurity. By analyzing transaction data and user behavior, anomalies can be identified, and potential security breaches can be detected early, preventing financial losses and protecting sensitive information.

>>> ***Natural Language Processing (NLP):*** NLP, a subfield of data science, enables machines to understand and process human language. It powers virtual assistants, chatbots, and language translation systems, enhancing communication and productivity across various domains.

>>> ***Environmental Monitoring and Sustainability:*** Data science is instrumental in environmental monitoring and sustainability efforts. By analyzing data from remote sensors

and satellites, data scientists can monitor climate change, track deforestation, and manage natural resources more efficiently.

>>> ***Social Sciences and Policy Making***: Data science techniques are applied to analyze social data and gain insights into human behavior, opinion trends, and societal issues. Governments and policymakers use this information to develop evidence-based policies and address social challenges effectively.

Applications of Data Science:

>>> ***Recommender Systems:*** Online platforms, such as e-commerce websites, streaming services, and social media, employ data science to build recommender systems. These systems suggest products, movies, music, or content based on user preferences and behaviour, enhancing user engagement and satisfaction.

>>> ***Financial Analytics:*** In the financial sector, data science is used for risk assessment, credit scoring, fraud detection, and algorithmic

trading. Analyzing market data and financial indicators helps traders and investors make informed decisions.

>>> Image and Speech Recognition: Image and speech recognition systems, powered by data science and machine learning algorithms, have found applications in self-driving cars, medical diagnostics, and security surveillance.

>>> Healthcare Diagnostics: Data science enables the analysis of medical images, such as X-rays, MRIs, and CT scans, aiding in the early detection and diagnosis of diseases.

>>> Social Media Analysis: Data science is used to analyze social media data, understand user sentiment, detect trends, and measure the impact of marketing campaigns.

>>> Supply Chain Optimization: Data science optimizes supply chain management by predicting demand, improving inventory management, and reducing logistics costs.

>>> Smart Cities: Data science plays a crucial role in building smart cities, where data is leveraged to optimize traffic flow, manage energy consumption, and enhance public services.

>>> Sports Analytics: Sports teams and organizations use data science to analyze player performance, optimize strategies, and gain a competitive edge.

>>> Genomics and Biotechnology: Data science is employed in genomics research to analyze DNA sequences, understand genetic diseases, and develop personalized medicine.

In conclusion, data science is of paramount importance in today's data-driven world. Its applications span across industries and domains, touching nearly every aspect of modern life. By extracting valuable insights from data, data science empowers organizations and individuals to make data-driven decisions, fuel innovation, and solve complex problems. As the volume of data continues to grow exponentially, the role of data science will only become more crucial in shaping a better, data-enabled future.

1. Data Science in Various Industries

Data science has become a transformative force in various industries, revolutionizing the way businesses operate and make decisions. Its ability to extract valuable insights from data and drive data-driven strategies has led to widespread adoption across diverse sectors. In this article, we will explore how data science is applied in different industries and the impact it has had on their operations and outcomes.

A. Healthcare:

Data science has brought significant advancements to the healthcare industry. It enables the analysis of vast amounts of medical data, including electronic health records, medical imaging, and genomic data. Through machine learning algorithms, data science facilitates early disease detection, personalized treatment plans, and drug discovery.

Medical imaging analysis is one of the areas where data science has made a substantial impact. Algorithms can interpret X-rays, MRIs, and CT scans, aiding in the detection of diseases like cancer and identifying abnormalities. Additionally, data science plays a crucial role in predicting disease outcomes based on patient data, optimizing hospital workflows, and reducing healthcare costs.

B. Finance:

In the financial industry, data science is extensively used for risk assessment, fraud detection, and algorithmic trading. By analyzing historical financial data and market trends, data science models can predict risks and assess creditworthiness. This assists banks and financial institutions in making informed lending decisions and managing their portfolios more effectively.

Fraud detection is another critical application of data science in finance. Machine learning algorithms can detect anomalies in transaction patterns, helping identify fraudulent activities and minimizing financial losses.

C. Retail and E-commerce:

Data science has transformed the retail and e-commerce sectors by enabling personalized recommendations, supply chain optimization, and customer behavior analysis. Recommender systems use data on user preferences and past interactions to offer tailored product suggestions, enhancing the shopping experience and boosting customer loyalty.

Supply chain optimization involves predicting demand, improving inventory management, and optimizing logistics to reduce costs and enhance efficiency. Data science also helps retailers optimize pricing strategies, design targeted marketing campaigns, and identify emerging trends.

D. Marketing and Advertising:

Data science plays a vital role in marketing and advertising by analyzing customer behavior, sentiment analysis, and optimizing ad campaigns. Through data-driven insights, businesses can understand their target audience better, deliver personalized content, and improve conversion rates.

Sentiment analysis uses natural language processing (NLP) techniques to analyze social media posts, customer reviews, and online discussions to gauge public sentiment towards products, brands, or campaigns. This information helps marketers tailor their messaging and respond to customer feedback effectively.

E. Manufacturing:

Data science has revolutionized the manufacturing industry by facilitating predictive maintenance, quality control, and process optimization. Through sensor data and historical performance, predictive maintenance models can forecast equipment failures and schedule maintenance proactively, reducing downtime and increasing productivity.

Data science is also used for quality control by analyzing production data to identify defects and ensure products meet the desired standards. Moreover, process optimization involves using data science to streamline manufacturing processes, identify inefficiencies, and improve overall productivity.

F. Energy and Utilities:

In the energy and utilities sector, data science is applied to optimize energy consumption, improve grid management, and enhance renewable energy production. Smart meter data analysis helps in understanding energy usage patterns and designing energy-efficient solutions for consumers.

Grid management involves analyzing data from sensors and other sources to ensure a stable and reliable power supply. Additionally, data science enables the prediction of energy demand, optimizing energy distribution and reducing waste.

G. Transportation and Logistics:

Data science is transforming the transportation and logistics industry by enabling route optimization, demand forecasting, and asset management. By analyzing data from GPS devices, weather forecasts, and traffic patterns, data science models can recommend the most efficient routes for transportation, reducing delivery times and fuel consumption.

Demand forecasting helps logistics companies anticipate customer needs and allocate resources accordingly, optimizing their operations. Data science also enhances asset management by predicting maintenance needs and ensuring the optimal utilization of vehicles and equipment.

H. Agriculture:

Data science is making significant strides in agriculture by enabling precision farming, crop yield prediction, and pest detection. By analyzing data from sensors, satellites, and drones, data science models provide farmers with insights into soil health, moisture levels, and crop health.

Crop yield prediction assists in making informed decisions about planting schedules and resource allocation. Additionally, data science helps in early detection of pests and diseases, allowing farmers to implement targeted interventions and minimize crop losses.

In conclusion, data science is driving transformative changes across various industries, enabling data-driven decision-making, optimizing operations, and unlocking new possibilities for growth and innovation. From healthcare and finance to retail, manufacturing, and agriculture, data science is reshaping the way businesses operate, offering valuable insights and solutions to complex challenges. As technology advances and data volumes continue to grow, the importance of data science in industries will only increase, propelling us towards a more data-driven and efficient future.

Chapter 2: The Data Science Workflow

1. Data Collection and Data Sources

Data collection is a fundamental step in the data science process, where relevant and reliable data is gathered from various sources to be used for analysis, insights generation, and decision-making. The quality and suitability of the data collected significantly impact the accuracy and validity of the results obtained through data analysis. In this article, we will explore data collection methods, types of data sources, and considerations for ensuring data integrity and usefulness.

Data Collection Methods:

>>> Surveys and Questionnaires: Surveys and questionnaires are common methods of data collection, particularly in social sciences and market research. They involve structured questions that are administered to a sample of respondents to gather their opinions, preferences, or experiences.

>>> ***Interviews:*** Interviews are conducted in a one-on-one or group setting to collect qualitative data from participants. They provide in-depth insights and allow researchers to explore complex topics and nuances.

>>> ***Observations:*** Observational data collection involves systematically observing and recording behaviours, events, or phenomena without directly interfering with the subjects. It is often used in ethnographic research and behavioural studies.

>>> ***Sensors and Internet of Things (IoT) Devices:*** With the rise of the Internet of Things, sensors and IoT devices have become valuable sources of data. They collect real-time data on various environmental and operational parameters, such as temperature, humidity, motion, and location.

>>> ***Web Scraping:*** Web scraping is a technique used to extract data from websites automatically. It allows data scientists to gather

large amounts of structured and unstructured data from the internet for analysis.

>>> *Social Media Data:* Social media platforms generate vast amounts of data through user interactions, posts, and comments. Data from social media can provide valuable insights into customer sentiments, trends, and brand perception.

>>> *Transactional Data:* Transactional data, often found in databases, records details of business transactions, online purchases, and financial transactions. This data is commonly used for business intelligence and analysis.

>>> *Secondary Data:* Secondary data refers to existing data that was collected for a different purpose but can be reused for new analyses. Publicly available datasets, government reports, and academic publications are examples of secondary data sources.

Types of Data Sources:

>>> *Structured Data:* Structured data is organized and formatted in a predefined manner, usually in tabular form with rows and columns. Databases and spreadsheets are common sources of structured data. This type of data is easy to analyze and query.

>>> ***Unstructured Data:*** Unstructured data lacks a predefined structure and is typically found in the form of text, images, audio, and video files. Social media posts, emails, and documents are examples of unstructured data sources. Analyzing unstructured data often requires advanced natural language processing (NLP) and computer vision techniques.

>>> ***Semi-Structured Data:*** Semi-structured data has some level of structure, such as XML or JSON files, but does not conform to a strict schema like structured data. Web pages, log files, and certain types of documents are sources of semi-structured data.

>>> ***Time-Series Data:*** Time-series data records observations over time at regular intervals. It is commonly used in applications where data points are captured sequentially,

such as financial markets, weather data, and sensor readings.

>>> Geospatial Data: Geospatial data contains location-based information and is often represented using coordinates, such as latitude and longitude. It is utilized in mapping, navigation, and location-based services.

Considerations for Data Collection:

>>> Data Relevance and Objectives: Data collection should be aligned with the objectives of the analysis or research. Collecting irrelevant or extraneous data can lead to wasted resources and confusion during analysis.

>>> Data Quality: Data quality is crucial for reliable and accurate analysis. Data scientists must ensure that the collected data is accurate, complete, and free from errors or inconsistencies.

>>> Data Privacy and Ethics: When collecting data, it is essential to consider data privacy and ethical implications. Personal and sensitive data must be handled with care, and appropriate consent should be obtained from participants.

>>> ***Sample Size and Representativeness:*** In survey-based data collection, the sample size and representativeness of the sample are critical factors. A representative sample helps generalize the findings to the larger population.

>>> ***Data Security:*** Data security is essential to protect sensitive information from unauthorized access, tampering, or data breaches.

>>> ***Data Cleaning and Preprocessing:*** Raw data often requires cleaning and preprocessing to remove duplicates, handle missing values, and transform the data into a suitable format for analysis.

>>> ***Data Storage and Management:*** Proper data storage and management practices are essential to ensure data accessibility, integrity, and compliance with data regulations.

In conclusion, data collection is a foundational step in the data science process. The choice of data collection methods and sources significantly impacts the outcomes of data analysis and decision-making. It is essential for data scientists to carefully plan and execute data collection, considering factors such as data relevance, quality, privacy, and representativeness. By collecting and leveraging data effectively, data scientists can unlock valuable insights and drive meaningful outcomes in various domains and industries.

1. Data Cleaning and Preprocessing

Data cleaning and preprocessing are fundamental steps in the data science workflow. They involve the process of transforming raw, messy, and inconsistent data into a clean, organized, and suitable format for analysis. These preparatory steps are essential as the quality and accuracy of the data significantly impact the reliability and effectiveness of the subsequent data analysis and modeling stages. In this article, we will explore the concepts of data cleaning and preprocessing in-depth, highlighting their significance and the techniques employed to ensure high-quality data.

Data Cleaning:

Data cleaning, also known as data cleansing or data scrubbing, refers to the process of identifying and rectifying errors, inconsistencies, and inaccuracies in the data. Raw data often contains various issues, such as missing values, outliers, duplicates, and formatting discrepancies. These issues can arise from various sources, including data entry errors, data integration from multiple sources, and sensor malfunctions. Data cleaning aims to correct or remove these anomalies to ensure data integrity and improve the accuracy of analyses and models.

A. Handling Missing Values:

Missing values are one of the most common challenges in real-world datasets. They can occur when data is not recorded, lost during data transfer, or simply not applicable. Dealing with missing values is crucial to avoid biased analyses or erroneous conclusions. Different strategies can be employed to handle missing values, such as:

>> ***Deleting Rows:*** If the missing values are few and do not significantly affect the dataset's integrity, the rows containing missing values can be removed. However, this approach can lead to loss of valuable information.

>> ***Imputation:*** Missing values can be replaced with estimated values based on statistical techniques like mean, median, or mode imputation. More advanced imputation methods, like regression imputation or K-nearest neighbors (KNN) imputation, can be used for more accurate estimates.

B. Removing Duplicates:

Duplicates can occur due to data entry errors or data integration from multiple sources. Duplicate records can lead to skewed analyses and inflated results. Identifying and removing duplicates is essential for data consistency and accuracy.

C. Outlier Detection and Treatment:

Outliers are data points that significantly deviate from the majority of the data. Outliers can arise due to measurement errors or rare events. They can have a disproportionate impact on statistical analyses and machine learning models. Data cleaning involves identifying outliers and deciding how to handle them, which can involve removal, transformation, or assigning a special treatment to the outliers.

D. Handling Inconsistent Data:

Inconsistent data occurs when the same entity is represented in multiple ways (e.g., different spellings, capitalizations, or abbreviations). Data cleaning involves standardizing and resolving such inconsistencies to ensure data consistency and accurate analyses.

Data Preprocessing:

Data preprocessing involves the preparation of data for further analysis and modeling. It includes a series of transformations and manipulations to make the data more amenable to algorithms and improve the performance of data-driven tasks.

A. Data Transformation:

Data transformation is a crucial step in data preprocessing, as many machine learning algorithms assume that the data follows a specific distribution or structure. Common data transformations include:

>> Feature Scaling: Scaling features to a similar range prevents certain features from dominating the learning process, especially in algorithms sensitive to feature scales, like K-nearest neighbors and gradient descent-based methods.

>> ***Normalization:*** Normalizing data to have a mean of zero and a standard deviation of one ensures that features have comparable scales and are centered around zero.

>> ***Log Transformation***: Log-transforming skewed data can help achieve a more symmetric distribution and stabilize variance, making it more suitable for certain algorithms.

B. Encoding Categorical Variables:

Machine learning algorithms often require numerical inputs, but real-world datasets often include categorical variables (e.g., gender, color, country). Data preprocessing involves encoding categorical variables into numerical representations, such as one-hot encoding or label encoding.

>> ***One-Hot Encoding:*** In one-hot encoding, each category is represented by a binary vector, where only one element is 1 and the others are 0. This technique prevents the algorithm from assigning ordinal relationships to categories.

>> Label Encoding: Label encoding assigns a unique integer to each category, but it can introduce an ordinal relationship between categories, which may not be appropriate for certain algorithms.

C. Feature Engineering:

Feature engineering involves creating new features from existing ones to enhance the predictive power of the data. It is a creative and domain-specific process that requires a deep understanding of the problem and data. Feature engineering can involve mathematical operations, domain knowledge-based transformations, or creating interaction terms between features.

D. Dimensionality Reduction:

Dimensionality reduction techniques are used to reduce the number of features while preserving essential information. High-dimensional data can be computationally expensive and may lead to overfitting in machine learning models. Principal Component

Analysis (PCA) and t-distributed Stochastic Neighbor Embedding (t-SNE) are popular dimensionality reduction techniques.

E. Data Splitting:

Before applying machine learning algorithms, the data is split into training and testing sets. The training set is used to train the model, and the testing set is used to evaluate its performance. Proper data splitting helps assess the model's generalization capabilities and avoid overfitting.

In conclusion, data cleaning and preprocessing are critical steps in the data science workflow. Data cleaning ensures that the data is accurate and free from errors, while data preprocessing prepares the data for analysis and modeling. By addressing missing values, removing duplicates, handling outliers, and transforming features, data cleaning and preprocessing ensure that data science models and algorithms can produce meaningful and reliable insights. The success of data-driven tasks, such as predictive modeling and machine learning, heavily depends on the quality and preparation of the data, making data cleaning and preprocessing indispensable steps in the journey from raw data to valuable insights.

1. Exploratory Data Analysis (EDA)

Exploratory Data Analysis (EDA) is a critical step in the data science process that involves the systematic exploration, visualization, and summary of data to gain insights, identify patterns, detect anomalies, and generate hypotheses. EDA serves as the foundation for subsequent data modeling and analysis, helping data scientists understand the structure and characteristics of the data, make informed decisions on data preprocessing, and design appropriate statistical or machine learning approaches for further investigation. In this article, we will delve into the concept of

Exploratory Data Analysis, its objectives, techniques, and its significance in the data science workflow.

Objectives of Exploratory Data Analysis:

A. Data Understanding:

EDA allows data scientists to get a clear understanding of the data at hand. It involves examining the size of the dataset, the number of features, the data types, and the distribution of values in each feature.

A. Data Quality Assessment:

EDA helps identify and assess the quality of the data. Data quality issues, such as missing values, outliers, and inconsistencies, can significantly impact the reliability of subsequent analyses. EDA enables data scientists to make informed decisions on data cleaning and preprocessing.

A. Data Visualization:

EDA utilizes various graphical representations to visualize the data, making patterns and trends more apparent. Visualization aids in identifying relationships between variables, spotting outliers, and gaining insights that may not be evident from numerical summaries alone.

A. Feature Selection:

EDA assists in selecting relevant features for analysis. Identifying which features are most informative or have the strongest relationships with the target variable is crucial for building accurate predictive models.

A. Hypothesis Generation:

EDA can generate hypotheses or initial assumptions about the relationships between variables. These hypotheses can guide further analysis and experimentation to validate or refute them.

Techniques used in Exploratory Data Analysis:

A. Summary Statistics:

Summary statistics provide a concise overview of the data's central tendency, variability, and distribution. Common summary statistics include mean, median, mode, variance, standard deviation, minimum, and maximum values.

A. Data Visualization:

Data visualization techniques present data in graphical forms, making it easier to understand patterns and relationships. Common visualization techniques include:

>> ***Histograms:*** Histograms display the frequency distribution of a continuous variable, helping to understand its distribution and detect outliers.

>> ***Box Plots:*** Box plots show the distribution of data in terms of quartiles, median, and outliers. They are useful for comparing distributions across different groups or categories.

>> ***Scatter Plots:*** Scatter plots visualize the relationship between two continuous variables, helping identify correlations or trends.

>> Bar Charts: Bar charts display the distribution of categorical variables, making it easy to compare frequencies between categories.

>> Heatmaps: Heatmaps show the correlation matrix between variables, highlighting the strength and direction of relationships.

A. ***Data Grouping and Aggregation:***

Grouping data by specific categories or time intervals allows data scientists to gain insights into trends and patterns in different subsets of the data.

A. ***Dimensionality Reduction:***

Techniques like Principal Component Analysis (PCA) or t-distributed Stochastic Neighbour Embedding (t-SNE) can be used for dimensionality reduction, helping visualize high-dimensional data in lower dimensions.

Significance of Exploratory Data Analysis:

A. Data Quality Assessment:

EDA helps identify data quality issues early in the data science workflow. By detecting missing values, outliers, or inconsistencies, data scientists can take appropriate actions, such as data cleaning or imputation, to ensure the integrity of the data.

A. Feature Engineering:

EDA insights can guide feature engineering, where new features are created from existing ones to improve model performance. Understanding relationships between features helps in identifying relevant interactions and transformations.

A. ***Model Selection:***

EDA provides critical insights into the data distribution and relationships, enabling data scientists to select appropriate models. For example, if the data exhibits a linear relationship, linear regression might be a suitable choice.

A. ***Outlier Detection:***

EDA can identify outliers, which are data points that significantly deviate from the majority of the data. Handling outliers appropriately is essential for building robust models.

A. ***Decision-Making:***

EDA provides data-driven insights that aid decision-making in various domains. Whether it's business strategy, product development, or policy-making, EDA helps stakeholders understand the data context and make informed choices.

A. Identifying Data Limitations:

EDA highlights the limitations and biases present in the data. Data scientists can adjust their analysis and interpretations accordingly, ensuring the results are valid within the context of the data.

A. Hypothesis Generation:

EDA generates initial hypotheses, which can be tested using statistical tests or further analysis. These hypotheses guide the research process and prevent data analysis from being purely exploratory without any specific direction.

In conclusion, Exploratory Data Analysis is a crucial step in the data science process, allowing data scientists to gain a comprehensive understanding of the data, identify patterns, and make informed decisions on data preprocessing and modeling. The insights derived from EDA guide subsequent data analysis, model building, and decision-making, ensuring that data-driven solutions are robust and effective. By combining summary statistics, data visualization, and dimensionality reduction techniques, EDA empowers data scientists to unearth valuable insights from the data, driving innovation and problem-solving across various domains.

1. Feature Engineering

Feature engineering is a critical process in the field of data science and machine learning that involves the creation and selection of relevant and informative features from raw data. Features are the individual variables or attributes in a dataset that serve as inputs to machine learning algorithms for making predictions or classifications. Feature engineering aims to extract meaningful information, reduce noise, and enhance the performance of machine learning models by transforming or creating new features that are more suitable for the task at hand. In this article, we will explore the concept of feature engineering in-depth, its objectives, techniques, and its significance in building accurate and robust predictive models.

Objectives of Feature Engineering:

A. Improving Model Performance:

The primary objective of feature engineering is to enhance the performance of machine learning models. By providing the models with more informative and relevant features, the models can better capture the underlying patterns and relationships in the data, leading to improved predictions or classifications.

A. ***Handling Missing Data:***

Feature engineering can address the issue of missing data by imputing or creating new features to fill in the gaps. Proper handling of missing data ensures that the model can make use of all available information and prevents the loss of valuable data points.

A. ***Reducing Dimensionality:***

In many real-world datasets, the number of features can be high, leading to the "curse of dimensionality." Feature engineering techniques can reduce the dimensionality of the data by selecting the most relevant features or by creating new features that capture the essence of the data more efficiently.

A. Dealing with Non-Linearity:

Some machine learning algorithms assume linearity in the data, while real-world data is often non-linear. Feature engineering can transform the data or create new features to address non-linearity, making the data more amenable to linear models.

Techniques used in Feature Engineering:

A. Encoding Categorical Variables:

Machine learning algorithms typically work with numerical data, and real-world datasets often include categorical variables (e.g., gender, color, country). Feature engineering involves encoding categorical variables into numerical representations to enable their use in models. Two common techniques are:

>> ***One-Hot Encoding:*** In one-hot encoding, each category is represented by a binary vector, where only one element is 1 and the others are 0. This technique prevents the algorithm from assigning ordinal relationships to categories.

>> ***Label Encoding:*** Label encoding assigns a unique integer to each category, but it can introduce an ordinal relationship between

categories, which may not be appropriate for certain algorithms.

B. Feature Scaling:

Feature scaling ensures that all features have comparable scales, preventing certain features from dominating the learning process, especially in algorithms sensitive to feature scales, like K-nearest neighbors and gradient descent-based methods. Common scaling techniques include min-max scaling and standardization.

C. Binning:

Binning involves grouping continuous numerical values into bins or intervals. This process can transform numerical features into categorical features, making them more robust to outliers and variations in the data.

D. Log Transformation:

Log transformation is used to address data with a skewed distribution. Taking the logarithm of a feature can transform it into a more symmetric distribution, making it more suitable for certain algorithms that assume normality.

E. Polynomial Features:

For linear models, adding polynomial features can capture non-linear relationships between features and the target variable. By creating interactions and higher-order terms, polynomial features allow models to capture more complex patterns in the data.

F. Interaction Features:

Interaction features are created by combining two or more existing features to represent the combined effect. For example, in a dataset with height and weight, an interaction feature like BMI (Body Mass Index) can be created by dividing weight by height squared.

G. Feature Extraction from Text and Images:

For unstructured data like text and images, feature engineering involves extracting meaningful information and converting it into numerical representations. Techniques like Bag-of-Words, Term Frequency-Inverse Document Frequency (TF-IDF), and Word Embeddings are used for text data. For images, convolutional neural networks (CNNs) can be used to extract features.

H. Significance of Feature Engineering:

Model Performance Improvement: Feature engineering significantly impacts model performance. By selecting the most informative features and transforming the data into a more suitable format, models can better capture complex relationships in the data, leading to more accurate predictions.

>> Overfitting Prevention: Feature engineering helps prevent overfitting, where a model performs well on the training data but poorly on unseen data. By reducing noise and focusing on relevant features, overfitting is minimized, ensuring the model's generalization capabilities.

>> Resource Efficiency: Properly engineered features can lead to more

resource-efficient models. Reduced dimensionality and fewer irrelevant features decrease the computational burden and memory requirements of the model.

>> Domain Knowledge Utilization: Feature engineering enables data scientists to incorporate domain knowledge into the modeling process. By creating features that reflect domain-specific insights, the model can benefit from expert knowledge and improve its performance.

>> Interpretability: Feature engineering can enhance the interpretability of machine learning models. When features are carefully crafted, the model's predictions become more understandable and actionable, making it easier to explain

the model's decision-making process to stakeholders.

In conclusion, feature engineering is a fundamental aspect of the data science and machine learning workflow. It plays a pivotal role in transforming raw data into informative and relevant features that enable models to make accurate predictions and classifications. Through various techniques like encoding categorical variables, feature scaling, binning, and creating interaction features, data scientists can optimize the data for specific algorithms, improve model performance, and ensure the generalization of the model to unseen data. By harnessing domain knowledge and employing creative techniques, feature engineering empowers data scientists to unlock the full potential of their data and build robust and accurate predictive models across diverse domains and applications.

Chapter 3: Tools and Technologies in Data Science

1. Introduction to Python for Data Science

Python has emerged as a popular and powerful programming language for data science due to its simplicity, versatility, and an extensive ecosystem of libraries and tools. Data science is the interdisciplinary field that involves extracting knowledge and insights from data, and Python serves as a flexible and efficient language to handle the data manipulation, analysis, and visualization tasks that are essential in this domain.

A. Python's Key Features for Data Science

Python boasts several key features that make it well-suited for data science applications. First and foremost, Python is an easy-to-learn language, making it accessible to beginners and experts alike. Its clear and readable syntax allows data scientists to write concise and efficient code, promoting code reusability and maintainability. Furthermore, Python is an interpreted language, which means that it doesn't require compilation and allows for faster development cycles.

One of the primary reasons for Python's popularity in data science is its extensive library support. Libraries like NumPy, Pandas, and Matplotlib provide robust data structures, tools for data manipulation, and visualization capabilities, respectively. Additionally, Python integrates seamlessly with other languages like C and R, enabling data scientists to leverage their existing code and take advantage of specialized libraries.

B. Essential Libraries for Data Science in Python

a. NumPy: NumPy is the fundamental package for numerical computing in Python. It provides powerful array objects that allow for efficient operations on large datasets. NumPy's array-oriented computing and broadcasting capabilities significantly speed up numerical computations, making it a cornerstone of data science workflows.

b. Pandas: Pandas is a versatile library that offers data structures like DataFrame and Series, which facilitate data manipulation and analysis. DataFrames are akin to spreadsheets and SQL tables, allowing data scientists to perform operations like filtering, grouping, merging, and joining data effortlessly.

c. Matplotlib: Data visualization is crucial for understanding data and communicating insights effectively. Matplotlib, a 2D plotting library, enables data scientists to create various types of plots, such as line charts, bar plots, histograms, and scatter plots. Its customizable nature allows for the creation of publication-quality visualizations.

d. Seaborn: Seaborn is built on top of Matplotlib and provides a higher-level interface for creating attractive statistical graphics. It simplifies the process of generating complex visualizations like pair plots, heatmaps, and violin plots, helping data scientists explore and communicate data patterns more effectively.

C. Data Cleaning and Preprocessing

Data scientists often deal with messy and unstructured data, making data cleaning and preprocessing critical steps in the data science pipeline. Python, along with libraries like Pandas, provides efficient tools for these tasks.

Data cleaning involves handling missing values, dealing with duplicate entries, and correcting inconsistent data. Pandas offers functions like dropna(), duplicated(), and fillna() that aid in addressing these issues.

Preprocessing involves transforming raw data into a format suitable for analysis and modeling. This step may include scaling numeric features, encoding categorical variables, and splitting data into training and testing sets. Libraries like Scikit-learn, which work seamlessly with Pandas, provide a wide range of preprocessing tools.

4. Exploratory Data Analysis (EDA)

EDA is a crucial phase in data science that involves visually exploring and summarizing the main characteristics of a dataset. Python's libraries, especially Pandas and Matplotlib, make EDA efficient and insightful.

Data scientists can use Pandas to calculate summary statistics, generate histograms, and create box plots to gain initial insights into data distributions and potential outliers. Matplotlib and Seaborn can be employed to create various plots to visualize relationships between variables, uncover patterns, and identify correlations.

5. Data Modeling and Machine Learning

Python is an ideal language for implementing machine learning algorithms and building predictive models. The Scikit-learn library is a prominent choice for machine learning in Python as it provides an extensive array of tools for classification, regression, clustering, and more.

Scikit-learn's unified API makes it easy to experiment with various algorithms without significant code changes. Data scientists can follow a standardized workflow to split data, train models, tune hyperparameters, and evaluate performance.

6. Deep Learning with TensorFlow and PyTorch

For more complex and deep neural networks, Python offers two dominant frameworks: TensorFlow and PyTorch. TensorFlow, developed by Google, and PyTorch, developed by Facebook, provide high-level abstractions for building and training deep learning models.

These frameworks are used in cutting-edge applications like image recognition, natural language processing, and reinforcement learning. Their flexibility, computational efficiency, and strong community support have made them essential tools for data scientists working on advanced machine learning projects.

In conclusion, Python's versatility, ease of use, and extensive library support have made it a go-to language for data scientists worldwide. From data manipulation and visualization to advanced machine learning and deep learning, Python's ecosystem of libraries continues to evolve, empowering data scientists to extract valuable insights from data effectively. Whether you're a beginner or an experienced data scientist, Python provides the tools and resources to tackle the challenges of the ever-expanding field of data science.

1. Key Python Libraries: NumPy, Pandas, and Matplotlib

Python's popularity in the data science community owes much to its extensive ecosystem of libraries. Three of the most fundamental and widely used libraries in this domain are NumPy, Pandas, and Matplotlib. Together, they form a powerful trio that allows data scientists to efficiently manipulate, analyze, and visualize data, making them essential tools for any data science project.

1. NumPy: Numerical Computing in Python

NumPy, short for "Numerical Python," is the foundation of numerical computing in Python. It provides a powerful array object, numpy.ndarray, along with an assortment of functions to perform operations on these arrays efficiently. The key advantage of NumPy is its ability to handle large datasets and perform vectorized operations, which significantly speeds up computations compared to traditional Python lists.

a. Arrays and Vectorized Operations: NumPy arrays are

homogeneous, multidimensional collections of data, and they can be of any dimension. This makes NumPy well-suited for representing matrices, tensors, and other complex data structures. The real power of NumPy lies in its support for vectorized operations, where mathematical operations are performed on entire arrays, rather than individual elements, using optimized C code under the hood. This results in faster and more concise code.

b. Universal Functions (ufuncs): NumPy provides a wide range of universal functions that work element-wise on arrays. These ufuncs enable operations like addition, subtraction, multiplication, division, and more. Moreover, NumPy includes trigonometric, logarithmic, and statistical functions, which are essential for data analysis and scientific computations.

c. ***Broadcasting:*** Broadcasting is a powerful feature of NumPy that allows arrays with different shapes to be operated together. This feature eliminates the need for explicit loops and enables elegant and concise expressions of complex operations.

1. Pandas: Data Manipulation Made Easy

Pandas is a versatile and powerful library for data manipulation and analysis in Python. It introduces two primary data structures: Series and DataFrame. These structures make it easy to handle structured and tabular data, offering a more intuitive and efficient way to manage datasets.

a. ***Series:*** A Series is a one-dimensional array-like object that can hold data of any type. It is equipped with a labeled index, allowing for easy data access and alignment. Pandas Series can be thought of as a mix between a Python list and a dictionary, combining the compactness of an array with the flexibility of labeled data.

b. ***DataFrame:*** A DataFrame is a two-dimensional tabular data structure, resembling a spreadsheet or SQL table. It consists of rows and columns, where each column can hold different data types. DataFrame is particularly well-suited for analyzing real-world datasets as it provides a powerful set of methods for data filtering, selection, grouping, merging, and reshaping.

c. Data Alignment and Handling Missing Data: One of the key advantages of Pandas is its built-in handling of missing data. Pandas Series and DataFrame objects align data based on their labels automatically, even when performing operations. Missing data is represented as NaN (Not a Number), and Pandas offers various methods to deal with these missing values, like dropna() and fillna().

1. Matplotlib: Data Visualization in Python

Matplotlib is a comprehensive library for creating static, interactive, and publication-quality visualizations in Python. It offers a wide range of plot types, customization options, and visualization styles, making it an essential tool for data scientists and researchers who need to communicate their findings visually.

a. Pyplot Interface: Matplotlib provides two main interfaces: the pyplot interface and the object-oriented interface. The pyplot interface, inspired by MATLAB, offers a simple way to create basic plots with minimal code. It's commonly used for quick data visualization and exploration.

b. Object-Oriented Interface: The object-oriented interface provides more control and flexibility over the plot elements. Data scientists can create and modify plots by directly interacting with the Figure, Axes, and other plot components. This approach is particularly useful for creating complex, customized visualizations.

c. Types of Plots: Matplotlib supports a wide range of plot types, including line plots, scatter plots, bar plots, histograms, pie charts, heatmaps, and many more. It allows users to visualize relationships between variables, distributions, trends, and patterns in the data effectively.

1. Integration and Interoperability

One of the key advantages of these libraries is their seamless integration. NumPy arrays serve as the foundation for Pandas DataFrames, enabling efficient data processing and analysis. Both NumPy and Pandas are supported by Matplotlib, allowing for smooth data visualization without data conversion or manipulation.

Furthermore, the integration with other libraries extends the capabilities of this trio. For example, Scikit-learn, a popular machine learning library, works effortlessly with NumPy arrays and Pandas DataFrames, enabling data scientists to seamlessly train and evaluate machine learning models. Additionally, Pandas integrates well with databases, making it a versatile tool for data ingestion and retrieval from various sources.

In conclusion, NumPy, Pandas, and Matplotlib are foundational libraries in the Python ecosystem, serving as essential tools for data scientists and researchers. NumPy's numerical computing capabilities, combined with Pandas' data manipulation and analysis features, create a robust framework for handling datasets of varying complexities. Matplotlib's visualization capabilities complement the data analysis process, allowing data scientists to present their findings effectively.

This trio of libraries enables data scientists to perform a wide range of tasks, from data preprocessing and exploratory analysis to building predictive models and creating insightful visualizations. With their user-friendly interfaces and extensive documentation, NumPy, Pandas, and Matplotlib continue to empower data scientists to tackle real-world data challenges and gain meaningful insights from their data.

1. Virtual Environments for Data Science Projects

Virtual environments are a critical tool for data scientists to manage and isolate the dependencies of their projects. A virtual environment allows you to create a self-contained environment with its own set of Python libraries, avoiding conflicts between different projects. This capability is particularly valuable in data science, where various projects often require different library versions or configurations. In this in-depth explanation, we will explore the concept of virtual environments, their benefits, and how to create and manage them in data science projects.

1. Understanding Virtual Environments

In Python, a virtual environment is a directory that contains a specific Python interpreter and its own set of installed packages. When you create a virtual environment, it essentially creates a separate space for your project, keeping it isolated from other Python installations and libraries on your system. This isolation ensures that the dependencies for one project don't interfere with another.

Virtual environments are especially important for data science projects because they often involve numerous libraries with different versions and dependencies. By creating a virtual environment for each project, you can maintain consistency and reproducibility across different development and deployment environments.

1. Benefits of Virtual Environments

a. Dependency Isolation: Data science projects often rely on numerous external libraries, each with its specific version requirements. In a virtual environment, you can install the exact versions of the required libraries, preventing conflicts and ensuring that your project runs consistently regardless of the system it's deployed on.

b. Reproducibility: Virtual environments enhance reproducibility by providing a complete snapshot of the project's dependencies. This allows you to recreate the exact environment used during development, making it easier to share your project with others and replicate results.

c. Easy Collaboration: When collaborating with other data scientists or developers, virtual environments ensure that everyone is working with the same library versions and configurations, reducing the chances of compatibility issues.

d. Sandboxing: Virtual environments act as sandboxes for your projects, providing a safe space to experiment with different libraries and configurations without affecting your system-wide Python installation.

3. Creating Virtual Environments

Python provides built-in support for creating and managing virtual environments through the "venv" module (Python 3.3+). To create a virtual environment for your data science project, you can follow these steps:

a. Install Python: Ensure you have Python 3.3 or higher installed on your system. You can check your Python version by running python—version or python3—version in the terminal.

b. Creating a Virtual Environment: Open a terminal or command prompt, navigate to your project directory, and execute the following command to create a virtual environment named "env" (you can choose any name you prefer):

```
python3 -m venv env
```

This command will create a new "env" directory in your project folder containing the isolated Python environment.

c. Activating the Virtual Environment: To activate the virtual environment, use the appropriate command based on your operating system:

- ***On Windows:***

```
env\Scripts\activate
```

- ***On macOS and Linux:***

```
source env/bin/activate
```

When the virtual environment is activated, your terminal prompt will change, indicating that you are now working within the virtual environment.

4. Installing Libraries in the Virtual Environment

Once the virtual environment is active, any Python packages you install will be specific to that environment, and they won't affect your system-wide Python installation. You can use the pip command to install libraries as usual:

```
pip install pandas numpy matplotlib scikit-learn
```

These packages will be installed in the "env" directory, and your project will have access to them.

5. Deactivating the Virtual Environment

When you're done working on your data science project and want to switch back to your system's Python environment, you can deactivate the virtual environment by running the following command:

```
deactivate
```

After deactivating, your terminal prompt will revert to its original state, indicating that you are now using the system-wide Python installation.

6. Managing Virtual Environments with Requirements.txt

In data science projects, it's common to have a list of specific library versions that the project depends on. To maintain a clear record of these dependencies, you can create a "requirements.txt" file that lists all the libraries and their versions.

To generate the "requirements.txt" file, activate your virtual environment and use the following command:

pip freeze > requirements.txt

This will create a text file named "requirements.txt" in your project folder with a list of all the installed libraries and their versions.

7. Using Requirements.txt for Dependency Management

Whenever you or someone else needs to set up the project's environment, they can do so by creating a new virtual environment and then installing the required libraries from the "requirements.txt" file:

```
python3 -m venv env
source env/bin/activate
pip install -r requirements.txt
```

This ensures that the virtual environment is set up with the exact dependencies specified in the "requirements.txt" file.

In conclusion, virtual environments are an indispensable tool for data scientists working on multiple projects with different dependencies. They provide isolation, reproducibility, and ease of collaboration, all essential factors for successful data science projects. By creating and managing virtual environments, data scientists can confidently experiment with libraries, share projects with others, and maintain consistency across different environments, making their data science workflows more efficient and manageable.

Unit II: The Mathematics of Data Science

The Mathematics of Data Science is the foundational framework that underpins the entire field of data science, providing the tools and techniques necessary to extract valuable insights and knowledge from vast amounts of data. It serves as the backbone of data science, enabling professionals to make informed decisions, predictions, and recommendations in various domains. This discipline relies on a combination of mathematical concepts, statistics, probability theory, linear algebra, calculus, and optimization methods, among others, to handle data efficiently and accurately.

At the core of The Mathematics of Data Science lies the concept of statistics, which involves the collection, analysis, interpretation, and presentation of data. Statistics allows data scientists to draw meaningful conclusions from datasets, identify patterns, and make predictions based on observed patterns. Descriptive statistics summarizes the main features of a dataset, such as mean, median, and standard deviation, while inferential statistics enables making inferences or predictions about a population based on a sample.

Another critical aspect of this field is probability theory, which deals with the likelihood of events occurring. It plays a pivotal role in data science, particularly in tasks like machine learning, where algorithms leverage probabilities to make decisions and predictions. By understanding probabilities, data scientists can model uncertainties and quantify the reliability of their conclusions.

Linear algebra serves as the mathematical foundation for manipulating and representing data in various forms, such as matrices and vectors. Many data science algorithms are formulated using linear algebra, making it an essential tool for tasks like dimensionality reduction, regression analysis, and deep learning. Moreover, linear algebra facilitates understanding the relationships between different variables in a dataset and helps identify hidden patterns.

Calculus, with its branches of differentiation and integration, is vital for optimizing models and functions. Optimization algorithms are widely used in data science to find the best solution to a problem, whether it's finding optimal parameters for a machine learning model or maximizing efficiency in resource allocation. Data scientists leverage techniques from calculus to fine-tune models and enhance their performance.

In addition to these fundamental mathematical concepts, data scientists employ advanced techniques like numerical methods and computational algorithms to handle complex mathematical operations efficiently. These numerical methods are crucial for solving equations, approximating solutions, and handling real-world data, which often involves noise and uncertainty.

Graph theory is another significant area of mathematics utilized in data science. It provides tools to represent and analyze the relationships and connections within data, especially in the context of networks and social graphs. Graph algorithms help identify clusters, influencers, and patterns within interconnected datasets.

The Mathematics of Data Science extends beyond these core concepts and encompasses various other mathematical tools and techniques. Time series analysis, for instance, enables data scientists to handle temporal data and forecast future trends. Bayesian statistics, on the other hand, is valuable for dealing with uncertain information and updating beliefs based on new evidence.

In conclusion, The Mathematics of Data Science is a multifaceted discipline that encompasses a wide range of mathematical concepts and tools. It provides data scientists with the means to extract meaningful insights, make accurate predictions, and optimize models for various applications. By combining statistics, probability theory, linear algebra, calculus, optimization, and other mathematical techniques, data scientists can tackle complex problems and leverage the power of data to drive informed decision-making in the modern world. A strong understanding of these mathematical foundations is essential for any aspiring data scientist, as it forms the backbone of this rapidly evolving and transformative field.

Chapter 4: Foundations of Mathematics for Data Science

1. Number Systems and Arithmetic Operations

Number Systems and Arithmetic Operations form the fundamental concepts of mathematics that deal with representing and manipulating quantities. These concepts are essential in various fields, from basic calculations to complex scientific and engineering applications. Understanding number systems and arithmetic operations is crucial for building a solid mathematical foundation and for advancing in more advanced mathematical and computational disciplines.

>>> Number Systems:

A number system is a way of representing quantities using symbols or digits. Different number systems exist, but the most commonly used ones are the decimal (base-10), binary (base-2), octal (base-8), and hexadecimal (base-16) systems.

A. ***Decimal Number System:***

The decimal system uses ten digits from 0 to 9 to represent numbers. Each position in a decimal number has a value equal to a power of 10. For example, the number "352" in the decimal system can be expanded as (3 * 10^2) + (5 * 10^1) + (2 * 10^0).

A. ***Binary Number System:***

The binary system uses two digits, 0 and 1, to represent numbers. Each position in a binary number corresponds to a power of 2. Binary is widely used in computer science because computers process and store data in binary form. For instance, the binary number "1101" is (1 * 2^3) + (1 * 2^2) + (0 * 2^1) + (1 * 2^0) in decimal.

A. Octal Number System:

The octal system uses eight digits from 0 to 7 to represent numbers. Each octal position corresponds to a power of 8. Although octal is not as prevalent as binary or decimal, it finds applications in certain computer systems and programming.

A. Hexadecimal Number System:

The hexadecimal system uses sixteen digits, 0 to 9, and A to F (representing values 10 to 15) to represent numbers. Each hexadecimal position corresponds to a power of 16. Hexadecimal is commonly used in computer science, especially for representing memory addresses and binary data more succinctly.

Converting between number systems involves understanding the place value of each digit and performing arithmetic operations specific to the given base. This skill is important in computer programming, digital electronics, and cryptography, among other areas.

>>> Arithmetic Operations:

Arithmetic operations involve manipulating numbers using basic mathematical operations: addition, subtraction, multiplication, and division.

A. Addition:

Addition combines two or more numbers to get a sum. It is denoted by the "+" symbol. Addition is commutative (changing the order of numbers does not affect the result) and associative (the grouping of numbers does not change the result). For example, 3 + 5 = 8, and (2 + 4) + 6 = 2 + (4 + 6) = 12.

A. ***Subtraction:***

Subtraction is the process of finding the difference between two numbers. It is denoted by the "-" symbol. Subtraction is not commutative (changing the order of numbers changes the result). For example, 7 - 4 = 3, but 4 - 7 = -3.

A. ***Multiplication:***

Multiplication is repeated addition or grouping of numbers. It is denoted by the "*" symbol. Multiplication is commutative and associative. For instance, 4 * 3 = 3 * 4 = 12, and (2 * 3) * 4 = 2 * (3 * 4) = 24.

A. ***Division:***

Division is the process of sharing or distributing a quantity into equal parts. It is denoted by the "/" symbol. Division is not commutative, and division by zero is undefined. For example, 12 / 4 = 3, but 4 / 12 = 1/3.

In addition to these basic arithmetic operations, other operations like exponentiation and modular arithmetic are also significant.

>>> Exponentiation:

Exponentiation is the process of raising a number (base) to a power (exponent). It is denoted by the "^" symbol. For instance, 2^3 = 2 * 2 * 2 = 8, and 10^2 = 10 * 10 = 100. Exponentiation is essential in mathematical modeling, engineering, and scientific calculations.

>>> Modular Arithmetic:

Modular arithmetic deals with the remainder when a number is divided by another number (modulus). It is denoted by "mod" or "%". Modular arithmetic finds applications in computer science, cryptography, and number theory. For example, 7 mod 3 = 1, and 10 mod 4 = 2.

Order of Operations: When performing arithmetic operations, following the correct order of operations is crucial to obtain the right result. The order of operations is usually remembered using the acronym PEMDAS:

- P: Parentheses first
- E: Exponents (i.e., powers and roots, etc.)
- MD: Multiplication and Division (from left to right)
- AS: Addition and Subtraction (from left to right)

By adhering to this order, we ensure that calculations are performed correctly, especially in complex expressions.

In conclusion, Number Systems and Arithmetic Operations are fundamental mathematical concepts that play a crucial role in various fields, including computer science, engineering, physics, and finance. Understanding different number systems allows for efficient representation and conversion of data, while arithmetic operations enable us to perform basic calculations and solve complex problems. Having a solid grasp of these concepts lays the groundwork for more advanced mathematical and computational endeavors, making them indispensable tools for anyone working with numbers and data.

1. Sets, Relations, and Functions

Sets, Relations, and Functions are fundamental concepts in mathematics that play a crucial role in various fields, including algebra, analysis, and computer science. They provide a powerful framework for organizing and understanding the relationships between elements and sets of data. Let's explore each of these concepts in detail:

Sets:

A set is a collection of distinct objects or elements, and it is denoted by listing its elements within curly braces. For example, the set of natural numbers less than 5 can be represented as {1, 2, 3, 4}. Sets can contain any type of elements, such as numbers, letters, or even other sets. The cardinality of a set is the number of elements it contains.

Sets are characterized by their properties and operations:

A. Subset:

A set A is said to be a subset of another set B if all elements of A are also elements of B. We denote this relationship as $A \subseteq B$. For example, if A = {1, 2} and B = {1, 2, 3}, then A is a subset of B.

A. Proper Subset:

A set A is considered a proper subset of another set B ($A \subset B$) if A is a subset of B, but A and B are not equal. In the example above, A is a proper subset of B if B = {1, 2, 3, 4}.

A. Union:

The union of two sets A and B, denoted as $A \cup B$, is the set of all elements that belong to A, B, or both. For example, if A = {1, 2, 3} and B = {3, 4, 5}, then $A \cup B$ = {1, 2, 3, 4, 5}.

A. Intersection:

The intersection of two sets A and B, denoted as $A \cap B$, is the set of elements that are common to both A and B. Using the sets from the previous example, $A \cap B$ = {3}.

A. Complement:

The complement of a set A, denoted as A', is the set of all elements that are not in A but belong to a specific universal set U. For example, if U is the set of all natural numbers, and A = {1, 2, 3}, then A' = {4, 5, 6, ...}.

Sets serve as the basis for more complex mathematical structures and concepts, such as functions and relations.

Relations:

A relation is a connection or association between elements of two or more sets. Relations can be represented using ordered pairs, where the first element of the pair is from one set, and the second element is from another set. A relation between sets A and B can be denoted as $R \subseteq A \times B$, where $A \times B$ is the Cartesian product of A and B, which consists of all possible ordered pairs (a, b), where $a \in A$ and $b \in B$.

Various types of relations exist, each having its properties:

A. Reflexive Relation:

A relation R on a set A is reflexive if every element of A is related to itself. In other words, $(a, a) \in R$ for all $a \in A$.

A. Symmetric Relation:

A relation R on a set A is symmetric if for every $(a, b) \in R$, $(b, a) \in R$.

A. Transitive Relation:

A relation R on a set A is transitive if for every $(a, b) \in R$ and $(b, c) \in R$, then $(a, c) \in R$.

A. Equivalence Relation:

An equivalence relation is a relation that is reflexive, symmetric, and transitive. Equivalence relations partition a set into disjoint subsets (equivalence classes) that share common characteristics.

A. *Partial Order Relation:*

A partial order relation is a relation that is reflexive, antisymmetric (if (a, b) ∈ R and (b, a) ∈ R, then a = b), and transitive. It establishes a partial ordering of elements in a set.

Relations are essential in various fields, such as graph theory, databases, and formal languages. They provide a means to model connections between elements and can be used to analyze and solve real-world problems.

Functions:

A function is a special type of relation that assigns exactly one output (value) to each input (element) from a set. In other words, for every input, there is a unique output. A function is denoted as f: A → B, where A is the domain (the set of input values) and B is the codomain (the set of possible output values). The notation f(a) represents the output (image) of the element a ∈ A.

Functions can be represented using various methods, such as graphs, tables, or algebraic expressions. *They are characterized by several properties:*

A. **Domain:**

The domain of a function is the set of all valid input values for which the function is defined.

A. **Codomain:**

The codomain is the set of all possible output values of the function.

A. **Range:**

The range of a function is the set of all output values obtained when all elements of the domain are evaluated.

A. ***Injectivity (One-to-One):***

A function is injective if each element in the domain maps to a distinct element in the codomain. In other words, $f(a) = f(b)$ if and only if $a = b$.

A. ***Surjectivity (Onto):***

A function is surjective if every element in the codomain has at least one pre-image in the domain.

A. ***Bijectivity:***

A function is bijective if it is both injective and surjective. A bijective function establishes a one-to-one correspondence between the elements of the domain and the codomain.

Functions are ubiquitous in mathematics and its applications. They are used to model relationships between variables, perform transformations, and analyze various phenomena. In calculus, functions are central to understanding rates of change, derivatives, and integrals.

In conclusion, Sets, Relations, and Functions are foundational concepts in mathematics with broad applications in various disciplines. Sets provide a means to organize and group elements, while relations establish connections between elements from different sets. Functions, being a special type of relation, map elements from one set to another, enabling the modeling and analysis of real-world problems. Understanding these concepts is essential for building a strong mathematical background and for advancing to more advanced topics in mathematics and other fields such as computer science, physics, and engineering.

1. Logic and Propositional Calculus

Logic is the branch of mathematics and philosophy that deals with reasoning and the principles of valid argumentation. It provides a formal framework for understanding how information is processed and how conclusions are drawn from given premises. Propositional calculus, also known as propositional logic, is a fundamental part of logic that focuses on the study of propositions and their relationships, using symbolic representations and logical operators. It is widely used in computer science, mathematics, philosophy, and artificial intelligence to reason about statements and construct complex arguments.

Propositions:

In propositional calculus, a proposition is a declarative statement that is either true or false but not both. Propositions are represented using symbols, typically capital letters, and are often connected by logical operators to form compound propositions. For example, "The sun rises in the east" is a proposition because it is a definite statement with a clear truth value. In contrast, "What time is it?" is not a proposition since it does not have a definite truth value.

Logical Operators:

Logical operators are symbols used to connect propositions and form compound propositions. The three most fundamental logical operators in propositional calculus are:

A. Negation (¬):

The negation of a proposition p, denoted as ¬p, is the opposite of p. It is true if p is false, and false if p is true. For example, if p is "It is raining," then ¬p is "It is not raining."

A. Conjunction (∧):

The conjunction of two propositions p and q, denoted as p ∧ q, is true only when both p and q are true. Otherwise, it is false. For example, if p is "It is sunny," and q is "It is warm," then p ∧ q is "It is sunny and warm."

A. Disjunction (∨):

The disjunction of two propositions p and q, denoted as p ∨ q, is true when at least one of p and q is true. It is false only when both p and q are false. For example, if p is "It is raining," and q is "It is snowing," then p ∨ q is "It is raining or snowing."

Compound Propositions:

Compound propositions are formed by combining propositions using logical operators. The resulting compound proposition's truth value depends on the truth values of its component propositions and the logical operator used.

A. Conjunction (AND):

The compound proposition p ∧ q is true only when both p and q are true. If either p or q (or both) is false, then p ∧ q is false.

A. Disjunction (OR):

The compound proposition p ∨ q is true when at least one of p and q is true. It is false only when both p and q are false.

A. Negation (NOT):

The compound proposition $\neg p$ is true when p is false, and false when p is true.

Compound propositions can become more complex by combining multiple logical operators, creating truth tables to evaluate all possible combinations of truth values for the component propositions.

Truth Tables:

A truth table is a tabular representation of all possible combinations of truth values for a compound proposition. It allows us to determine the truth value of the compound proposition for each combination of truth values of its components. For example, let's consider the compound proposition $p \lor (q \land \neg r)$. If p, q, and r can take on either true (T) or false (F) as truth values, the truth table for this compound proposition would look like:

pQrq ∧ ¬rp ∨ (q ∧ ¬r)

TTTFT

TTFTT

TFTFT

TFFTT

FTTFF

FTFFF

FFTFF

FFFFF

By using truth tables, we can systematically evaluate compound propositions and determine their truth values for all possible scenarios.

Logical Equivalences:

Logical equivalences are important relationships between compound propositions. Two propositions are said to be logically equivalent if they always have the same truth value, regardless of the truth values of their component propositions. Logical equivalences are denoted using the double arrow symbol (⇔).

Some common logical equivalences include:

- ***Commutative Laws:***

  $p \land q \Leftrightarrow q \land p$ (AND is commutative)
  $p \lor q \Leftrightarrow q \lor p$ (OR is commutative)

- ***Associative Laws:***

  $(p \land q) \land r \Leftrightarrow p \land (q \land r)$ (AND is associative)
  $(p \lor q) \lor r \Leftrightarrow p \lor (q \lor r)$ (OR is associative)

- ***Distributive Laws:***

  $p \land (q \lor r) \Leftrightarrow (p \land q) \lor (p \land r)$
  $p \lor (q \land r) \Leftrightarrow (p \lor q) \land (p \lor r)$

- ***De Morgan's Laws:***

$\neg(p \land q) \Leftrightarrow \neg p \lor \neg q$ (Negation of AND)

$\neg(p \lor q) \Leftrightarrow \neg p \land \neg q$ (Negation of OR)

Logical equivalences are valuable for simplifying complex compound propositions and expressing them in more concise and manageable forms.

Applications:

The study of logic and propositional calculus has practical applications in various fields:

A. Computer Science:

Logic forms the basis of digital circuit design, programming, and algorithm analysis. Logical operators and truth tables are essential in Boolean algebra and Boolean logic, which underlie digital logic circuits in computers and electronic devices.

A. Philosophy:

Logic is a crucial tool in philosophy for analyzing and evaluating arguments and reasoning. It helps philosophers identify fallacies and construct valid arguments to support their claims.

A. Artificial Intelligence:

Logical reasoning is a significant component of artificial intelligence, where computers are programmed to follow logical rules to make decisions and perform tasks.

A. Mathematics:

Logical principles are used to construct proofs in various mathematical disciplines, such as algebra, calculus, and discrete mathematics.

In conclusion, logic and propositional calculus provide a formal framework for reasoning and making deductions based on given premises. By studying propositions, logical operators, truth tables, and logical equivalences, we can analyze complex statements and construct valid arguments. The applications of logic extend across various fields, making it an essential and versatile tool for understanding and solving problems in diverse domains.

Chapter 5: Linear Algebra for Data Scientists

1. Vectors and Matrices

Vectors and matrices are fundamental concepts in linear algebra, a branch of mathematics that deals with vector spaces and linear transformations. These concepts play a crucial role in various fields, including physics, engineering, computer graphics, and data science. Understanding vectors and matrices is essential for solving problems involving multiple variables, transformations, and systems of linear equations.

Vectors:

A vector is a mathematical object that represents both magnitude and direction. In its simplest form, a vector can be represented as an ordered list of numbers enclosed in parentheses or angular brackets. For example, a two-dimensional vector can be written as (x, y), where x and y are the components of the vector along the x and y axes, respectively.

Vectors can also be represented as column matrices, where each element of the vector is placed in a separate row. For example, the two-dimensional vector (x, y) can be represented as:

[x]

[y]

Vectors are often visualized as arrows in a coordinate system, with the arrow's length representing the vector's magnitude and the arrow's direction indicating its direction. Vectors can be added, subtracted, scaled (multiplied by a scalar), and subjected to various other operations.

Vector Operations:

A. Addition:

Vector addition involves adding the corresponding components of two vectors to produce a new vector. For example, if A = (a1, a2) and B = (b1, b2), then the sum of A and B, denoted as A + B, is (a1 + b1, a2 + b2).

A. Subtraction:

Vector subtraction involves subtracting the corresponding components of one vector from the corresponding components of another vector. If A = (a1, a2) and B = (b1, b2), then the difference between A and B, denoted as A - B, is (a1 - b1, a2 - b2).

A. *Scalar Multiplication:*

Scalar multiplication involves multiplying a vector by a scalar (a single number). For example, if A = (a1, a2) and k is a scalar, then the scalar multiplication kA is (ka1, ka2).

A. *Dot Product (Inner Product):*

The dot product of two vectors A and B, denoted as A · B, is the sum of the products of their corresponding components. For two-dimensional vectors A = (a1, a2) and B = (b1, b2), the dot product is given by A · B = (a1 * b1) + (a2 * b2).

A. *Cross Product (Outer Product):*

The cross product of two three-dimensional vectors A and B, denoted as A × B, is a new vector perpendicular to both A and B. The cross product is primarily used in three-dimensional vector spaces.

Matrices:

A matrix is a rectangular array of numbers or elements, arranged in rows and columns. Matrices are denoted by uppercase letters and are typically represented with square brackets. Each element of a matrix is specified by its row and column position. For example, a matrix A with m rows and n columns is written as A = [a_ij], where 1 ≤ i ≤ m and 1 ≤ j ≤ n.

[a_11 a_12 ... a_1n]
[a_21 a_22 ... a_2n]
[... ... ...]
[a_m1 a_m2 ... a_mn]

Matrices are used to represent and solve systems of linear equations, perform transformations, and solve problems involving multiple variables.

Matrix Operations:

A. Matrix Addition:

Matrix addition involves adding the corresponding elements of two matrices of the same dimensions. If A and B are two matrices of size m × n, the sum A + B is another matrix of size m × n, where each element is the sum of the corresponding elements of A and B.

A. Matrix Subtraction:

Matrix subtraction involves subtracting the corresponding elements of one matrix from the corresponding elements of another matrix. If A and B are two matrices of size m × n, the difference A - B is another matrix of size m × n, where each element is the difference between the corresponding elements of A and B.

A. Scalar Multiplication:

Scalar multiplication involves multiplying a matrix by a scalar, which multiplies each element of the matrix by the scalar value.

A. Matrix Multiplication:

Matrix multiplication is a binary operation that combines two matrices to produce a new matrix. It is essential to ensure that the number of columns in the first matrix is equal to the number of rows in the second matrix. If A is an m × n matrix and B is an n × p matrix, then the product AB is an m × p matrix, where each element is the dot product of the corresponding row of A and column of B.

A. Transpose:

The transpose of a matrix involves interchanging its rows and columns. If A is an m × n matrix, the transpose of A, denoted as A^T, is an n × m matrix obtained by flipping A over its main diagonal.

Applications:

Vectors and matrices have numerous applications in various fields:

A. Physics and Engineering:

Vectors are used to represent forces, velocities, and other physical quantities, while matrices are used to model and solve systems of linear equations in engineering problems.

A. *Computer Graphics:*

Vectors are used to represent points and directions in three-dimensional space, while matrices are used to perform transformations, such as rotation, translation, and scaling, on graphical objects.

A. *Data Science:*

Vectors and matrices are used to represent and manipulate data in machine learning and data analysis tasks. Matrices are particularly useful for storing and processing large datasets efficiently.

A. Linear Algebra:

Vectors and matrices are essential tools in linear algebra, where they are used to study vector spaces, linear transformations, and eigenvalues.

In conclusion, vectors and matrices are fundamental concepts in linear algebra that play a vital role in various mathematical and practical applications. Vectors represent magnitude and direction, while matrices represent arrays of numbers. Both vectors and matrices support various operations, such as addition, subtraction, scalar multiplication, and matrix multiplication. Understanding these concepts is crucial for solving problems involving multiple variables, transformations, and systems of linear equations, making them invaluable tools across diverse fields and disciplines.

1. Matrix Operations: Addition, Multiplication, and Inverse

Matrix operations are fundamental operations in linear algebra that involve manipulating matrices to solve various mathematical problems and practical applications. Matrices are rectangular arrays of numbers, and they play a crucial role in representing and solving systems of linear equations, performing transformations, and data analysis. Let's explore matrix addition, multiplication, and inverse in depth:

Matrix Addition:

Matrix addition involves adding corresponding elements of two matrices of the same dimensions. If we have two matrices A and B of the same size, with each matrix having m rows and n columns, their sum, denoted as A + B, is another matrix of size m × n. The sum is obtained by adding the elements of A and B at the same positions. Mathematically, if A = [a_ij] and B = [b_ij], then A + B = [a_ij + b_ij].

For example, consider the following two matrices:

A = [1 2

3 4]

B = [5 6

7 8]

Their sum A + B is:

A + B = [1+5 2+6

3+7 4+8]

= [6 8

10 12]

Matrix addition is commutative, which means that A + B = B + A. It is also associative, so (A + B) + C = A + (B + C) for matrices A, B, and C of the same size.

Matrix Multiplication:

Matrix multiplication is a more involved operation that combines two matrices to produce a new matrix. Unlike addition, matrix multiplication is not commutative, which means that AB ≠ BA in general. However, it is associative, so (AB)C = A(BC) for appropriate matrices A, B, and C.

Matrix multiplication is defined between an $m \times n$ matrix A and an $n \times p$ matrix B, where the number of columns in A is equal to the number of rows in B. The resulting product, denoted as AB, is an $m \times p$ matrix. Each element (i, j) of the product AB is obtained by taking the dot product of the i-th row of A and the j-th column of B.

Mathematically, if $A = [a_{ij}]$ is an $m \times n$ matrix and $B = [b_{ij}]$ is an $n \times p$ matrix, then $AB = [c_{ij}]$, where each element c_{ij} is given by:

$$c_{ij} = a_{i1} * b_{1j} + a_{i2} * b_{2j} + \dots + a_{in} * b_{nj}$$

For example, consider the following two matrices:

A = [1 2

3 4]

B = [5 6

7 8]

Their product AB is:

AB = [15 + 27 16 + 28

35 + 47 36 + 48]

= [19 22

43 50]

Matrix multiplication is crucial for performing transformations, solving systems of linear equations, and representing complex linear operations in a concise manner.

Matrix Inverse:

The inverse of a square matrix is a unique matrix that, when multiplied with the original matrix, produces the identity matrix. The identity matrix is a square matrix with ones on the main diagonal and zeros elsewhere. The inverse of a matrix A is denoted as A^(-1).

For a square matrix A to have an inverse, it must be non-singular or invertible. This means that its determinant (a scalar value calculated from the elements of the matrix) must be nonzero. If the determinant of A is zero, the matrix is singular, and it does not have an inverse.

The process of finding the inverse of a matrix can be done using various methods, such as Gaussian elimination, cofactor expansion, or the adjugate matrix method. Once the inverse is found, it can be used to solve systems of linear equations, among other applications.

Mathematically, if A is an $n \times n$ invertible matrix, then:

$$A * A^{(-1)} = A^{(-1)} * A = I$$

where I is the identity matrix of size $n \times n$.

Finding the inverse of a matrix is computationally intensive, especially for large matrices. In some cases, numerical methods are used to approximate the inverse for practical purposes.

Properties of Matrix Operations:

Matrix operations exhibit several important properties, some of which include:

A. ***Distributive Property:***

Matrix multiplication distributes over matrix addition, which means that A(B + C) = AB + AC for matrices A, B, and C with appropriate sizes.

A. ***Associative Property:***

Matrix multiplication is associative, so (AB)C = A(BC) for matrices A, B, and C of compatible sizes.

A. ***Scalar Multiplication Identity:***

The identity for scalar multiplication is 1, which means that 1A = A for any matrix A.

A. ***Transpose and Inverse Relationship:***

For an invertible matrix A, the inverse of its transpose is equal to the transpose of its inverse: (A^T)^(-1) = (A^(-1))^T.

Matrix operations, along with their properties, form the foundation of linear algebra and are extensively used in various fields, including physics, engineering, computer science, and statistics.

Applications:

Matrix operations have numerous applications in diverse fields:

A. ***Solving Systems of Linear Equations:***

Matrices can represent systems of linear equations, and matrix operations are used to solve these systems and find solutions for unknown variables.

A. ***Transformations and Graphics:***

Matrix operations are essential in computer graphics and

transformational geometry to manipulate images, perform rotations, scaling, and translation.

A. Data Analysis and Statistics:

Matrices are used to store and manipulate data in data science and statistics. Matrix operations, such as matrix multiplication, are applied in various statistical methods.

A. Physics and Engineering:

Matrices and matrix operations are used to represent and analyze physical systems, such as electrical circuits, mechanical systems, and quantum mechanics.

In conclusion, matrix operations are fundamental in linear algebra and play a crucial role in various mathematical and practical applications. Matrix addition combines corresponding elements of two matrices, matrix multiplication involves complex calculations that produce a new matrix, and matrix inverse is a unique matrix that, when multiplied with the original matrix, results in the identity matrix. Understanding these operations and their properties is essential for solving systems of equations, performing transformations, and analyzing data in a wide range of fields.

1. Eigenvalues and Eigenvectors

Eigenvalues and eigenvectors are important concepts in linear algebra that arise in the study of linear transformations and their effects on vectors. They play a crucial role in various fields, including physics, engineering, computer graphics, and data analysis. Understanding eigenvalues and eigenvectors provides valuable insights into the behavior of linear transformations and is widely used in solving practical problems.

Eigenvalues:

In linear algebra, an eigenvalue is a scalar value that represents how a linear transformation stretches or compresses a vector in a specific direction. When a linear transformation is applied to a vector, the resulting transformed vector might have the same direction as the original vector but possibly a different magnitude. An eigenvalue quantifies this scaling factor.

Mathematically, let's consider a linear transformation represented by a square matrix A. An eigenvalue λ and an eigenvector v of A satisfy the equation:

A * v = λ * v

where A is the matrix representing the linear transformation, v is the eigenvector, and λ is the eigenvalue.

To find the eigenvalues of a matrix, we solve the characteristic equation:

det(A - λ * I) = 0

where det() is the determinant, A is the matrix, λ is the eigenvalue, and I is the identity matrix of the same size as A. The solutions of the characteristic equation give the eigenvalues of the matrix.

Eigenvectors:

An eigenvector is a nonzero vector that remains in the same direction after a linear transformation, but its magnitude may change by a factor given by the corresponding eigenvalue. It represents the direction in which the linear transformation has a significant effect.

Returning to the equation A * v = λ * v, the vector v is the eigenvector corresponding to the eigenvalue λ. To find the eigenvectors corresponding to each eigenvalue, we solve the system of linear equations:

(A - λ * I) * v = 0

The solutions of this equation form the set of eigenvectors corresponding to the specific eigenvalue λ.

Geometric Interpretation:

The concept of eigenvalues and eigenvectors has a geometric

interpretation. In two dimensions, an eigenvector corresponds to a vector that remains on the same line after a linear transformation (scaling or rotation). The eigenvalue represents how much the eigenvector is scaled or compressed along that line.

In three dimensions, an eigenvector corresponds to a vector that remains on the same line (one-dimensional subspace) or plane (two-dimensional subspace) after the linear transformation. The eigenvalue represents the scaling factor or stretching along that line or plane.

In general, for higher dimensions, eigenvectors represent the directions in which the linear transformation acts as simple scaling operations. Eigenvalues provide the scaling factors along those directions.

Diagonalization of Matrices:

A square matrix A can be diagonalized if it has a full set of linearly independent eigenvectors. Diagonalization is the process of expressing the matrix A as a diagonal matrix D, where all off-diagonal elements are zero, and P is a matrix whose columns are the eigenvectors of A.

Mathematically, if A is a diagonalizable matrix, then:

$$A = P * D * P^{-1}$$

where P is the matrix containing eigenvectors of A, D is the diagonal matrix containing the corresponding eigenvalues on the main diagonal, and P^{-1} is the inverse of matrix P.

Diagonalization is particularly useful because it simplifies certain computations and makes the analysis of matrix transformations more straightforward.

Applications:

Eigenvalues and eigenvectors have various applications in different fields:

A. ***Principal Component Analysis (PCA):***

In data analysis, PCA uses eigenvectors to find the most significant directions (principal components) in the data and reduce its dimensionality while preserving most of its variance.

A. ***Structural Engineering:***

In structural analysis, eigenvalues are used to study the stability of structures, such as bridges and buildings.

A. Quantum Mechanics:

In quantum mechanics, eigenvectors are used to represent states of quantum systems, and eigenvalues represent the corresponding energy levels.

A. Computer Graphics:

In computer graphics, eigenvectors and eigenvalues are used to perform transformations, such as scaling and rotation of objects.

A. Machine Learning:

In various machine learning algorithms, such as Singular Value Decomposition (SVD) and Eigenface, eigenvectors and eigenvalues are used to analyze and process data.

Properties and Significance:

Eigenvalues and eigenvectors have several important properties:

A. ***Eigenvalues are Invariant:***

The eigenvalues of a matrix remain the same under similarity transformations, where a matrix A is replaced by P^(-1)AP for any invertible matrix P.

A. ***Linear Independence:***

Eigenvectors corresponding to distinct eigenvalues are linearly independent, meaning that none of them can be represented as a linear combination of the others.

A. ***Complex Eigenvalues:***

Eigenvalues and eigenvectors can be complex numbers, especially when dealing with non-real matrices.

A. ***Eigenvalues and Matrix Powers:***

The eigenvalues of A^n (the matrix A raised to the power n) are the eigenvalues of A, each raised to the power n.

A. ***Eigenvalues of Transpose and Inverse:***

The eigenvalues of the transpose of a matrix are the same as the eigenvalues of the original matrix. The eigenvalues of the inverse of a matrix are the reciprocals of the eigenvalues of the original matrix.

Eigenvalues represent the scaling factors, and eigenvectors represent the directions that remain unchanged under the transformation. They have various applications across diverse fields, including data analysis, physics, engineering, computer graphics, and machine learning. Understanding eigenvalues and eigenvectors enables us to analyze and solve problems involving linear transformations and systems of equations, making them invaluable tools in mathematical modeling and practical problem-solving.

Chapter 6: Multivariable Calculus: A Data Science Perspective

1. Partial Derivatives and Gradients

Partial derivatives and gradients are fundamental concepts in multivariable calculus, a branch of mathematics that deals with functions of multiple variables. They play a crucial role in various fields, including physics, engineering, economics, and machine learning. Understanding partial derivatives and gradients allows us to analyze how a function changes with respect to each of its variables and find the direction of steepest increase at a given point.

Partial Derivatives:

In calculus, a partial derivative measures the rate of change of a function with respect to one of its variables while holding the other variables constant. It allows us to analyze how a function responds to small changes in a specific direction. For functions of two or more variables, there can be multiple partial derivatives, each with respect to a different variable.

The notation for the partial derivative of a function f with respect to a variable x is $\partial f/\partial x$ or f_x. Similarly, for a function of two variables, f(x, y), the partial derivatives with respect to x and y are $\partial f/\partial x$ or f_x and $\partial f/\partial y$ or f_y, respectively.

To find the partial derivative of a function, we treat the variable of interest as the only variable and differentiate the function with respect to that variable, considering all other variables as constants.

Gradient:

The gradient is a vector representing the direction and magnitude of the steepest increase of a function at a given point in space. For a function f(x, y) of two variables, the gradient is denoted as ∇f or grad(f), and it is a vector with two components:

$$\nabla f = [\partial f/\partial x, \partial f/\partial y]$$

The gradient points in the direction of the steepest increase of the function at a given point and its magnitude gives the rate of change in that direction.

Geometric Interpretation:

The geometric interpretation of partial derivatives and gradients is essential for understanding their significance. For a function of two variables, $f(x, y)$, the partial derivative with respect to x, $\partial f/\partial x$, measures how the function changes concerning x when we move in the x-direction while keeping y constant. Similarly, $\partial f/\partial y$ measures how the function changes concerning y when we move in the y-direction while keeping x constant.

The gradient vector, ∇f, combines both partial derivatives and points in the direction of the steepest increase of the function at a given point (x, y). The magnitude of the gradient vector, $||\nabla f||$, gives the rate of change or slope of the function in that direction.

Interpreting Gradient Components:

The components of the gradient vector are crucial for understanding the direction and magnitude of the steepest increase of a function. If $\nabla f = [a, b]$, then:

A. ***When $a > 0$ and $b > 0$:***

The function increases in both the x and y directions. The steepest increase is in the direction of the vector [a, b].

A. ***When $a < 0$ and $b < 0$:***

The function decreases in both the x and y directions. The steepest decrease is in the direction of the vector [a, b].

A. ***When a and b have opposite signs:***

The function increases in one direction and decreases in the other. The steepest increase is in the direction of the vector [a, b], and the steepest decrease is in the direction of the vector [-a, -b].

A. When one component is zero:

The function remains constant in that direction.

Computing Partial Derivatives:

To compute the partial derivatives of a function, we differentiate the function with respect to each variable while keeping the other variables constant. For example, consider the function $f(x, y) = x^2 + 2xy + y^2$. To find $\partial f/\partial x$, we differentiate the function with respect to x, treating y as a constant:

$$\partial f/\partial x = d/dx\,(x^2 + 2xy + y^2) = 2x + 2y$$

Similarly, to find $\partial f/\partial y$, we differentiate the function with respect to y, treating x as a constant:

$$\partial f/\partial y = d/dy\,(x^2 + 2xy + y^2) = 2x + 2y$$

The gradient vector is then:

$\nabla f = [\partial f/\partial x, \partial f/\partial y] = [2x + 2y, 2x + 2y]$

Applications:

Partial derivatives and gradients have numerous applications in various fields:

A. ***Physics and Engineering:***

In physics and engineering, partial derivatives and gradients are used to analyze physical phenomena, such as heat distribution, fluid flow, and electrical fields.

A. **Economics:**

In economics, partial derivatives are used to analyze utility functions and production functions, while gradients are used in optimization problems, such as maximizing profit or minimizing cost.

A. ***Machine Learning:***

In machine learning, partial derivatives and gradients are used in optimization algorithms to find the minimum or maximum of a cost function and train models efficiently.

A. Computer Graphics:

In computer graphics, gradients are used for shading and lighting calculations to achieve realistic visual effects.

A. Statistics:

In statistics, gradients are used in maximum likelihood estimation and other optimization problems.

Chain Rule for Partial Derivatives:

The chain rule is a powerful tool for computing partial derivatives of composite functions. For a function $f(g(x, y), h(x, y))$ of two variables, the partial derivatives $\partial f/\partial x$ and $\partial f/\partial y$ can be calculated using the chain rule as follows:

$$\partial f/\partial x = (\partial f/\partial g) * (\partial g/\partial x) + (\partial f/\partial h) * (\partial h/\partial x)$$

$$\partial f/\partial y = (\partial f/\partial g) * (\partial g/\partial y) + (\partial f/\partial h) * (\partial h/\partial y)$$

The chain rule is especially useful when dealing with functions involving multiple variables and nested functions.

In conclusion, partial derivatives and gradients are powerful tools in multivariable calculus, providing insights into how functions change with respect to each variable and giving the direction of steepest increase. They find extensive applications in various fields, including physics, engineering, economics, machine learning, and computer graphics. Understanding these concepts allows us to analyze complex systems, optimize functions, and make informed decisions in practical problem-solving.

1. Optimization: Minimization and Maximization

Optimization is a fundamental concept in mathematics, engineering, economics, and various other fields that deals with finding the best possible solution among a set of alternatives. It involves maximizing or minimizing an objective function subject to certain constraints. The goal is to optimize the performance, efficiency, or effectiveness of a system or process. In this context, optimization can be broadly classified into two categories: minimization and maximization.

<u>Minimization:</u>

Minimization, as the name suggests, focuses on finding the lowest or smallest value of a given objective function. This type of optimization problem is prevalent in scenarios where we want to reduce costs, errors, or negative impacts. Examples include minimizing production costs in a manufacturing process, minimizing the time it takes to complete a task, or minimizing the energy consumption of a system.

In mathematical terms, given an objective function f(x) with variable(s) x, the minimization problem can be formally stated as finding the value(s) of x that make f(x) as small as possible, while satisfying certain constraints, if any. These constraints can be in the form of equations or inequalities that the variables must satisfy.

Minimization problems can be solved using various optimization techniques, such as gradient descent, simplex method, Newton's method, and many more, depending on the nature of the objective function and constraints. These methods iteratively update the values of variables to converge towards the optimal solution, where the objective function reaches its minimum value.

Maximization:

Conversely, maximization aims to find the highest or largest value of an objective function. This type of optimization problem is encountered when we want to maximize profits, utility, or benefits. Examples include maximizing the revenue generated by a business, maximizing the score in a game, or maximizing the efficiency of a system.

Similar to minimization, the maximization problem involves finding the value(s) of the variables that make the objective function f(x) as large as possible, while respecting any specified constraints. The mathematical formulation of the problem remains the same as in minimization, but the goal now is to find the values that lead to the maximum value of the objective function.

The techniques used to solve maximization problems are often analogous to those used in minimization problems. These methods aim to iteratively adjust the variable values to converge towards the optimal solution where the objective function reaches its maximum value.

Relationship Between Minimization and Maximization:

Minimization and maximization are intrinsically related, as many real-world problems involve optimizing different aspects.

Interestingly, problems that can be formulated as minimization can often be transformed into maximization problems and vice versa. This is achieved through the introduction of auxiliary variables or by manipulating the objective function and constraints.

For instance, if we have a minimization problem of minimizing f(x), we can create an equivalent maximization problem by considering the reciprocal of the objective function, i.e., maximizing 1/f(x). The optimal solutions for both the original minimization problem and its equivalent maximization problem will be the same.

Unconstrained and Constrained Optimization:

Optimization problems can further be classified into unconstrained and constrained optimization based on the presence of constraints.

In unconstrained optimization, there are no restrictions on the variables' values other than their natural domain. The goal is to find the optimal values of the variables that lead to the minimum or maximum value of the objective function without any limitations. Many classical optimization methods are designed for unconstrained problems and focus on exploring the function landscape to find critical points where the objective function is minimized or maximized.

Conversely, constrained optimization deals with problems where the variables must satisfy certain constraints while being optimized. These constraints could be linear or nonlinear equations and inequalities. Constrained optimization problems are often more challenging because the feasible region (the set of all valid variable values) is restricted by the constraints, and the optimal solution must lie within this feasible region.

Local and Global Optima:

In both minimization and maximization problems, it's essential to distinguish between local and global optima. A local optimum is a solution where the objective function reaches either a minimum or maximum value, but it may not be the best possible solution globally.

A global optimum, on the other hand, is the best solution among all possible solutions globally, regardless of local variations. Finding the global optimum can be more difficult, especially in complex and non-convex objective functions, as the optimization methods may get stuck in local optima.

The presence of multiple local optima and the challenge of identifying the global optimum make global optimization a fascinating and challenging area of research.

Optimization, in its two primary forms of minimization and maximization, plays a crucial role in various fields and applications. Whether it's minimizing costs, maximizing profits, or optimizing performance, the goal is to find the best possible solution under given constraints. Unconstrained and constrained optimization problems further add complexity to the process. The continuous advancement of optimization techniques and algorithms continues to enhance our ability to address real-world challenges and make better decisions in the face of complex systems and processes.

1. Applications of Multivariable Calculus in Data Science

Multivariable calculus is a branch of mathematics that deals with functions of several variables. In data science, where complex and high-dimensional datasets are analyzed, multivariable calculus plays a crucial role in understanding, modeling, and making predictions based on the data. It provides a powerful set of tools to handle multivariate relationships and optimize functions with multiple variables. Let's explore some of the key applications of multivariable calculus in data science.

A. Gradient Descent and Optimization:

Gradient descent is a popular optimization technique used in various machine learning algorithms to minimize a cost or loss function. In data science, the goal is often to find the optimal values of model parameters that best fit the data. Multivariable calculus is essential for calculating gradients, which represent the rate of change of a function concerning each parameter. By iteratively updating the model parameters in the direction of the negative gradient, gradient descent efficiently converges to the optimal solution.

B. Multivariate Regression Analysis:

Regression analysis is a fundamental data science technique used to model the relationship between one dependent variable and multiple independent variables. In multivariate regression, we have more than one predictor variable, making it a prime example of multivariable calculus application. The process involves estimating coefficients for each predictor variable and interpreting their impact on the dependent variable, which requires partial derivatives and understanding the multivariate relationship.

C. Principal Component Analysis (PCA):

PCA is a dimensionality reduction technique used to transform high-dimensional data into a lower-dimensional space while preserving most of the variance in the original data. Multivariable calculus is used in PCA to find the eigenvectors and eigenvalues of the covariance matrix of the data. These eigenvectors represent the principal components, and the eigenvalues determine the amount of variance explained by each component. The transformation process involves projecting the data onto the principal components, effectively reducing the dimensionality.

D. Gradient-Based Machine Learning Algorithms:

Many machine learning algorithms, such as support vector machines (SVM), neural networks, and deep learning models, rely on multivariable calculus to update the model parameters during the training process. Backpropagation in neural networks, for instance, uses partial derivatives to calculate gradients, which are then used to adjust the weights and biases in each layer to minimize the error.

E. Multivariate Probability Distributions:

In data science, understanding and modeling uncertainty are crucial. Multivariable calculus is used to define and analyze multivariate probability distributions, such as the multivariate normal distribution. These distributions allow data scientists to model the joint behavior of multiple variables and calculate probabilities associated with specific events or ranges of values.

F. Multivariable Integration in Statistics:

Multivariable calculus plays a role in statistics, particularly in calculating joint probabilities and expected values of multivariate random variables. Integration is used to compute probabilities and moments over regions defined by multiple variables. For instance, in Bayesian statistics, integrating over the joint posterior distribution helps estimate the expected value of model parameters.

G. Optimization of Neural Network Architectures:

Neural networks often have numerous hyperparameters, such as the number of layers, nodes per layer, and learning rate. Multivariable calculus techniques, such as gradient-based optimization and the chain rule, are used to optimize these hyperparameters and improve the network's performance. By finding the optimal configuration of hyperparameters, data scientists can build more efficient and accurate neural network architectures.

H. Multivariable Time Series Analysis:

In time series analysis, data scientists work with datasets where observations are recorded at multiple time points. Multivariable calculus concepts come into play when analyzing and modeling the relationships between different time series variables. Techniques like vector autoregression (VAR) models leverage multivariable calculus to capture dependencies between variables over time.

Multivariable calculus serves as a fundamental mathematical tool in data science, enabling professionals to analyze, model, and optimize multivariate relationships in complex datasets. Applications of multivariable calculus include gradient-based optimization, multivariate regression, PCA, and various machine learning algorithms. It also plays a crucial role in probability distributions, statistical integration, and time series analysis. As data science continues to evolve, multivariable calculus will remain a powerful ally in extracting valuable insights from diverse and high-dimensional datasets. Understanding these applications empowers data scientists to make informed decisions and build sophisticated models for real-world problem-solving.

Chapter 7: Probability and Statistics for Data Analysis

1. Probability Distributions: Discrete and Continuous

Probability distributions are a fundamental concept in statistics and probability theory that describe the likelihood of different outcomes or events occurring in a random experiment. They provide a mathematical framework to understand and model uncertainties in various real-world phenomena. Probability distributions can be broadly classified into two main types: discrete and continuous.

Discrete Probability Distributions:

Discrete probability distributions are used to model random variables that take on a finite or countable set of distinct values. The term "discrete" refers to the fact that the possible outcomes are separate and distinct, with no intermediate values between them. These distributions are characterized by probability mass functions (PMFs), which assign probabilities to each possible value of the random variable.

A classic example of a discrete probability distribution is the binomial distribution. It models the number of successes in a fixed number of independent Bernoulli trials, where each trial has two possible outcomes (success or failure) and a constant probability of success, denoted by "p." The binomial distribution is widely used in areas such as quality control, medical research, and opinion polls.

Another well-known discrete distribution is the Poisson distribution. It describes the number of events that occur in a fixed interval of time or space, given the average rate of occurrence. The Poisson distribution is often applied in fields like telecommunications, insurance, and queuing theory.

Discrete distributions have important properties, such as the sum of their probabilities being equal to 1. Additionally, moments, such as mean and variance, can be calculated to understand the central tendency and variability of the random variable.

Continuous Probability Distributions:

In contrast to discrete distributions, continuous probability distributions model random variables that can take on any value within a specified range or interval. The term "continuous" reflects the fact that the possible outcomes form an unbroken continuum, and individual outcomes may not be assigned a specific probability. Instead, probabilities are represented as areas under the probability density function (PDF) within intervals.

The normal distribution, also known as the Gaussian distribution, is one of the most well-known continuous probability distributions. It is characterized by its bell-shaped curve and is widely used in various fields due to the central limit theorem, which states that the sum of a large number of independent and identically distributed random variables approaches a normal distribution, regardless of the original distribution of the variables.

Another essential continuous distribution is the exponential distribution. It models the time between events in a Poisson process and is commonly used in reliability engineering, queueing theory, and survival analysis.

Continuous probability distributions have properties such as non-negative probabilities, where the total probability is obtained by integrating the PDF over the entire range of the random variable. Mean, variance, and other moments are calculated through integration, providing insights into the distribution's shape and spread.

Probability Density Function (PDF) vs. Probability Mass Function (PMF):

The distinction between PDF and PMF lies in the type of random variables they describe. For discrete random variables, the probability mass function (PMF) assigns probabilities to specific values of the random variable. In contrast, for continuous random variables, the probability density function (PDF) represents probabilities as densities across intervals of values.

In mathematical terms, the PMF of a discrete random variable X is denoted by P(X = x), where "x" represents a particular value, and P(X = x) gives the probability of X taking on that value. On the other hand, the PDF of a continuous random variable X is denoted by f(x), and the probability of X lying within a specific interval [a, b] is given by the integral of f(x) over that interval: ∫[a, b] f(x) dx.

Connection Between Discrete and Continuous Distributions:

Interestingly, there is a connection between certain discrete and continuous distributions. When the sample size of a discrete distribution becomes very large, it can approximate a continuous distribution. This is known as the continuity correction. For example, the binomial distribution with a large number of trials and a small probability of success per trial approaches the shape of a normal distribution. This approximation is valuable when dealing with continuous processes but having data generated from discrete events.

Probability distributions, whether discrete or continuous, are essential tools in understanding and modeling uncertainties in data and real-world phenomena. Discrete distributions are used when dealing with random variables that have a countable set of distinct values, while continuous distributions are employed for random variables with uncountably infinite possible values. The choice of the appropriate distribution depends on the nature of the data and the problem at hand.

The binomial distribution and the Poisson distribution are examples of discrete probability distributions, while the normal distribution and the exponential distribution are examples of continuous probability distributions. Each distribution has its unique properties and applications, allowing data scientists and statisticians to make informed decisions, analyze data, and draw meaningful insights from various datasets.

Understanding these probability distributions is essential for anyone working in fields that involve uncertainty, such as data science, finance, engineering, and many more.

1. Hypothesis Testing and Confidence Intervals

Hypothesis testing and confidence intervals are fundamental concepts in statistics that play a crucial role in making inferences about population parameters based on sample data. They are essential tools for decision-making, providing insights into the reliability of statistical conclusions and the uncertainty surrounding estimates. Let's explore these concepts in depth.

Hypothesis Testing:

Hypothesis testing is a systematic procedure used to test the validity of a claim or statement about a population parameter. It involves formulating two competing hypotheses, the null hypothesis (H0) and the alternative hypothesis (Ha). The null hypothesis represents the status quo or the assumption that there is no effect or difference, while the alternative hypothesis represents the researcher's assertion, suggesting that there is an effect or difference.

The hypothesis testing process involves the following steps:

A. *Formulating the Hypotheses:*

The null hypothesis (H0) is typically stated as a statement of no effect or no difference, while the alternative hypothesis (Ha) asserts the presence of an effect or difference.

A. *Choosing a Significance Level:*

The significance level (often denoted by α) is the probability of rejecting the null hypothesis when it is true. Commonly used significance levels are 0.05 and 0.01, representing a 5% and 1% chance of making a Type I error, respectively.

A. *Selecting a Test Statistic:*

The test statistic is a value computed from the sample data that measures the evidence against the null hypothesis. The choice of the test statistic depends on the nature of the hypothesis and the type of data being analyzed.

A. *Calculating the P-value:*

The p-value is the probability of observing a test statistic as extreme as the one calculated from the sample data, assuming that the null hypothesis is true. A small p-value suggests strong evidence against the null hypothesis, while a large p-value indicates weak evidence.

A. Making a Decision:

If the p-value is less than the chosen significance level (α), the null hypothesis is rejected in favor of the alternative hypothesis. Otherwise, there is not enough evidence to reject the null hypothesis, and it is retained.

A. Interpreting the Result:

The decision made through hypothesis testing helps draw conclusions about the population based on the sample data. However, it is crucial to understand the limitations and assumptions of the test used.

Hypothesis testing is widely used in various fields, such as medicine, social sciences, economics, and quality control, to assess the effectiveness of interventions, test hypotheses about population parameters, and make informed decisions.

Confidence Intervals:

Confidence intervals provide a range of plausible values within which the true population parameter is likely to lie with a certain level of confidence. They are constructed based on sample data and are used to quantify the uncertainty surrounding point estimates.

The construction of a confidence interval involves the following steps:

A. Choosing a Confidence Level:

The confidence level (often denoted by 1-α) represents the probability that the confidence interval contains the true population parameter. Commonly used confidence levels are 95% and 99%, implying that the interval will capture the parameter in 95% and 99% of repeated sampling, respectively.

A. ***Selecting a Point Estimate:***

A point estimate is a single value calculated from the sample data that serves as an estimate of the population parameter. For example, the sample mean is often used as a point estimate for the population mean.

A. ***Determining the Standard Error:***

The standard error is a measure of the variability of the point estimate due to sampling variability. It is typically calculated based on the sample size and the variability of the data.

A. *Calculating the Confidence Interval:*

The confidence interval is constructed around the point estimate by adding and subtracting the appropriate margin of error, which is based on the standard error and the chosen confidence level.

A. *Interpreting the Result:*

The confidence interval provides a range of values within which we are confident the true population parameter lies. The wider the confidence interval, the less precise the estimate, and vice versa.

Confidence intervals are useful for drawing conclusions about population parameters, such as means, proportions, or differences between means. They help researchers and analysts communicate the uncertainty associated with their estimates and provide a more informative representation of the data than point estimates alone.

Relationship Between Hypothesis Testing and Confidence Intervals:

Hypothesis testing and confidence intervals are closely related. In fact, they provide two different perspectives on the same statistical inference. When performing a two-tailed hypothesis test, the null hypothesis is rejected if the point estimate falls outside the corresponding confidence interval. Similarly, if the confidence interval includes the null value (e.g., zero), the null hypothesis is not rejected.

The confidence interval can be thought of as the set of all parameter values that would not be rejected in a hypothesis test with a specific level of significance. It gives a range of plausible values that are consistent with the data and the chosen confidence level.

Hypothesis testing and confidence intervals are essential tools in statistical analysis and decision-making. Hypothesis testing allows researchers to assess the validity of claims and make inferences about population parameters based on sample data. Confidence intervals provide a range of plausible values for the population parameter, taking into account the uncertainty in the estimate.

Together, these concepts provide a robust framework for drawing conclusions from data, making evidence-based decisions, and communicating the reliability of statistical findings. Understanding how to formulate hypotheses, calculate test statistics, and construct confidence intervals empowers researchers and analysts to draw meaningful insights from data and contribute to scientific advancements and informed decision-making processes.

Unit III: Python for Data Science

Python has emerged as one of the most popular programming languages for data science due to its simplicity, versatility, and an extensive ecosystem of libraries and tools. It provides a robust set of features that make it ideal for handling data manipulation, analysis, visualization, and machine learning tasks. In this context, "Python for Data Science" refers to the use of Python programming language and its associated libraries to extract insights and knowledge from data. Let's explore the key aspects of Python for data science in depth.

A. Data Manipulation and Analysis:

Python offers powerful libraries, such as NumPy and Pandas, that facilitate data manipulation and analysis. NumPy provides support for large, multi-dimensional arrays and matrices, along with a collection of mathematical functions to perform array operations efficiently. Pandas, on the other hand, offers data structures like Series and DataFrame, which allow for easy data organization, indexing, and filtering.

These libraries enable data scientists to handle large datasets with ease, perform data cleaning, aggregation, filtering, and transformation operations, making data preparation more manageable and efficient.

B. Data Visualization:

Data visualization is a critical aspect of data science, as it allows data scientists to communicate insights and patterns effectively. Python provides libraries like Matplotlib and Seaborn, which offer extensive functionality for creating static, interactive, and publication-quality visualizations.

Matplotlib allows users to create a wide range of plots, such as line plots, scatter plots, bar charts, histograms, and more. Seaborn, built on top of Matplotlib, offers additional functionalities, such as statistical data visualization, and provides aesthetically pleasing default styles.

C. Machine Learning:

Python's popularity for data science is greatly influenced by its excellent support for machine learning. Libraries like Scikit-learn provide a comprehensive set of tools for various machine learning tasks, including classification, regression, clustering, dimensionality reduction, and model evaluation.

Scikit-learn offers a user-friendly API, making it accessible to both beginners and experienced data scientists. It also provides various algorithms and tools for pre-processing data, feature extraction, and model selection, making the machine learning workflow more efficient.

D. Deep Learning:

Deep learning has gained significant traction in recent years, particularly in areas like computer vision, natural language processing, and speech recognition. Python has become a dominant language for deep learning due to the popularity of libraries like TensorFlow and PyTorch.

TensorFlow and PyTorch provide an easy-to-use interface for building and training complex neural networks. They offer support for both CPU and GPU acceleration, making it feasible to work with large datasets and models efficiently.

E. Data Integration and Web Scraping:

Python's versatility extends to data integration and web scraping. Libraries like Requests and BeautifulSoup enable data scientists to fetch data from various web sources, scrape websites, and extract valuable information for analysis.

These capabilities allow data scientists to gather data from different online repositories, APIs, and web services, enabling a more comprehensive and diverse analysis.

F. Interactivity and Collaboration:

Python's interactivity and ease of use, especially with Jupyter Notebooks, make it an ideal choice for collaborative data analysis and sharing results. Jupyter Notebooks provide an interactive environment where code, visualizations, and explanatory text can be combined, making it easier to explore and communicate findings.

Jupyter Notebooks support a wide range of data formats, including Markdown, HTML, and LaTeX, facilitating the creation of interactive and reproducible data reports.

G. Open Source Community and Ecosystem:

Python's open-source nature has contributed to the development of a vast ecosystem of libraries and tools for data science. The Python Package Index (PyPI) hosts thousands of libraries that cater to various data science needs, from statistical analysis to natural language processing.

The vibrant open-source community ensures continuous development, improvement, and support for these libraries, making Python an ever-evolving language for data science.

Python's popularity in the field of data science stems from its flexibility, ease of use, and extensive ecosystem of libraries and tools. It provides robust support for data manipulation and analysis through libraries like NumPy and Pandas, while Matplotlib and Seaborn offer powerful data visualization capabilities.

For machine learning and deep learning tasks, Python's Scikit-learn, TensorFlow, and PyTorch provide efficient and user-friendly APIs. The language's versatility also extends to data integration, web scraping, and interactivity through libraries like Requests, BeautifulSoup, and Jupyter Notebooks.

The collaborative nature of Python and its strong open-source community ensure that it will continue to be a leading choice for data science projects and research. Its user-friendly syntax and the availability of extensive documentation make it accessible to both beginners and experienced data scientists, empowering them to tackle complex data analysis challenges with ease and efficiency.

Chapter 8: Python Fundamentals

1. Variables and Data Types

Variables and data types are fundamental concepts in Python programming, as they form the building blocks for storing and manipulating data. In Python, a variable is a symbolic name that refers to a value or an object, and data types define the nature of the data stored in these variables. Understanding variables and data types is essential for effective programming and data manipulation in Python.

A. Variables in Python:

In Python, variables are used to store data values, such as numbers, strings, lists, or more complex objects. They act as placeholders that allow us to reference and manipulate data throughout the program. Unlike some other programming languages, Python is dynamically typed, meaning that you don't need to explicitly declare the data type of a variable before assigning a value to it. Instead, Python automatically infers the data type based on the assigned value.

Variable names in Python must follow certain rules:

- They can contain letters (a-z, A-Z), digits (0-9), and underscores (_).
- They must start with a letter or an underscore.
- They cannot be a reserved keyword, such as "if," "else," "while," etc.

For example, let's declare and assign values to some variables in Python:

```
# Integer variable
age = 25
# String variable
name = "John Doe"
# List variable
scores = [85, 92, 78, 95, 88]
# Dictionary variable
    person = {"name": "Alice", "age": 30}
```

B. Data Types in Python:

Python supports various data types that define the nature of the data stored in variables. Common data types in Python include:

- ***Numeric Types:*** These include integers, floating-point numbers, and complex numbers. Python automatically infers the appropriate numeric type based on the assigned value.

```
# Integer
age = 25
# Floating-point number
temperature = 98.6
# Complex number
    z = 3 + 4j
```

- ***Strings:*** Strings represent sequences of characters and are enclosed in either single quotes (' ') or double quotes (" ").

```
name = "Nibedita Sahu"
    message = 'Hello, World!'
```

- ***Boolean:*** Booleans represent the truth values True and False, which are used for logical operations and conditional expressions.

```
is_student = True

is_adult = False
```

- ***Lists:*** Lists are ordered collections of elements and can contain items of different data types.

```
scores = [85, 92, 78, 95, 88]
names = ["Nibe", "Dita", "NS"]
mixed_list = [10, "Nibedita", True, 3.14]
```

- ***Tuples:*** Tuples are similar to lists, but they are immutable, meaning their elements cannot be changed after creation.

```
coordinates = (10, 20)

RGB_color = (255, 128, 0)
```

- ***Dictionaries:*** Dictionaries are key-value pairs, where each value is associated with a unique key.

```
person = {"name": "Nibedita", "age": 20,
"occupation": "Programmer"}
```

- ***Sets:*** Sets are unordered collections of unique elements, and they do not allow duplicate values.

```
unique_numbers = {1, 2, 3, 4, 5}
```

- ***NoneType:*** The NoneType represents the absence of a value and is commonly used to initialize variables before assigning actual values.

```
result = None
```

Python's dynamic typing allows variables to change their data type during runtime:

```
x = 10 # Integer
x = "hello" # String
x = [1, 2, 3] # List
```

C. Type Conversion:

Python allows for explicit type conversion (also known as type casting) to convert variables from one data type to another. This is useful when you need to perform operations that are only valid for specific data types.

For example, converting a numeric string to an integer:

```
numeric_string = "123"

numeric_integer = int(numeric_string)
```

Similarly, converting an integer to a floating-point number:

```
x = 10

y = float(x)
```

It's important to note that not all conversions are valid, and attempting to convert incompatible data types may result in errors.

D. Checking Data Types:

You can check the data type of a variable using the type() function in Python:

```
age = 20
print(type(age)) # Output: <class 'int'>
name = "Nibedita Sahu"
print(type(name)) # Output: <class 'str'>
scores = [85, 92, 78, 95, 88]
print(type(scores)) # Output: <class 'list'>
```

Variables and data types are fundamental concepts in Python that enable programmers to store and manipulate data effectively. Variables act as symbolic names that refer to values or objects, while data types define the nature of the data stored in these variables.

Python supports a wide range of data types, including numeric types, strings, booleans, lists, tuples, dictionaries, sets, and NoneType. The dynamic typing feature allows variables to change their data type during runtime.

Type conversion allows programmers to explicitly convert variables from one data type to another when needed, and the type() function enables the checking of a variable's data type.

Understanding variables and data types is essential for successful Python programming and forms the foundation for working with data, performing calculations, and creating powerful and efficient algorithms.

1. Control Flow: Loops and Conditionals

Control flow is a fundamental concept in programming that governs the order of execution of statements and allows programmers to create flexible and efficient code. In Python, control flow is achieved through the use of loops and conditionals. Loops are used to execute a block of code repeatedly, while conditionals are used to make decisions and execute different blocks of code based on certain conditions. Understanding control flow is essential for writing structured and powerful programs in Python. Let's explore loops and conditionals in depth.

A. Conditionals in Python:

Conditionals, also known as decision-making statements, allow programmers to execute different blocks of code based on specified conditions. In Python, the primary conditional statement is the "if" statement, which follows the format:

```
if condition:

    # Code to execute if the condition is True
```

The condition is an expression that evaluates to either True or False. If the condition is True, the indented block of code following the "if" statement will be executed. If the condition is False, the block of code will be skipped.

```
x = 10
if x > 5:

    print("x is greater than 5")
```

In addition to the "if" statement, Python provides two other conditional statements: "else" and "elif" (short for "else if"). The "else" statement is used to specify an alternative block of code to execute when the condition of the "if" statement is False.

```
x = 3
if x > 5:
print("x is greater than 5")
else:
    print("x is not greater than 5")
```

The "elif" statement allows programmers to specify additional conditions to be tested when the preceding "if" and "elif" conditions are False. It can be used multiple times to chain multiple conditions.

```
x = 7
if x > 10:
print("x is greater than 10")
elif x > 5:
print("x is greater than 5 but not greater than
10")
else:

    print("x is less than or equal to 5")
```

Conditionals are powerful tools that enable programmers to implement decision-making logic in their programs, allowing for greater flexibility and control over program execution.

B. Loops in Python:

Loops are used to execute a block of code repeatedly until a certain condition is met. Python supports two types of loops: "for" loop and "while" loop.

- ***For Loop:***

The "for" loop is used to iterate over a sequence, such as a list, tuple, string, or range, and execute the block of code for each element in the sequence. The basic syntax of a "for" loop in Python is as follows:

```
for item in sequence:
    # Code to execute for each item in the sequence
```

Here, "item" represents the current element of the sequence being processed, and "sequence" is the iterable collection.

```
fruits = ["apple", "banana", "cherry"]
for fruit in fruits:
    print(fruit)
```

The "for" loop can also be used with the "range" function, which generates a sequence of numbers.

```
for i in range(5):
    print(i) # Output: 0 1 2 3 4
```

- ***While Loop:***

The "while" loop is used to repeatedly execute a block of code as long as a given condition is True. It is generally used when the number of iterations is not known beforehand.

```
count = 0
while count < 5:
print(count)

    count += 1
```

In this example, the loop will execute as long as the "count" variable is less than 5. The loop will terminate when the condition becomes False.

C. Loop Control Statements:

Python provides two control statements that can be used within loops to alter their behavior: "break" and "continue."

- The "break" statement is used to exit the loop prematurely when a certain condition is met. When the "break" statement is encountered, the loop is immediately terminated, and the program continues with the next statement after the loop.

```
fruits = ["apple", "banana", "cherry"]
for fruit in fruits:
if fruit == "banana":
break

    print(fruit) # Output: apple
```

- The "continue" statement is used to skip the current iteration of the loop and move to the next iteration when a certain condition is met.

```
numbers = [1, 2, 3, 4, 5]
for num in numbers:
if num % 2 == 0:
continue

    print(num) # Output: 1 3 5
```

D. Nested Loops and Conditionals:

Python allows the nesting of loops and conditionals, meaning that loops and conditional statements can be placed inside other loops or conditional blocks.

```
for i in range(3):
for j in range(2):

    print(i, j)
```

In this example, the "for" loop is nested inside another "for" loop, resulting in a total of six iterations.

Similarly, conditionals can be nested inside other conditionals:

```
x = 10
if x > 5:
if x < 15:

    print("x is between 5 and 15")
```

E. Infinite Loops:

Caution should be exercised when using loops to avoid infinite loops, where the loop's termination condition is never met. Infinite loops can lead to the program becoming unresponsive and may require forcibly terminating the program.

```
while True:

    # Infinite loop - avoid using this without a break condition
```

To prevent infinite loops, ensure that the loop's termination condition is achievable based on the logic of the program.

Control flow in Python, achieved through loops and conditionals, allows programmers to create flexible and powerful programs. Conditionals enable decision-making and allow for the execution of different blocks of code based on specified conditions. The "if," "else," and "elif" statements provide the necessary tools for implementing various decision-making logic.

Loops, on the other hand, enable the repetition of code blocks until a certain condition is met. "For" loops are used for iterating over sequences, while "while" loops are used for repeated execution based on a condition. The "break" and "continue" statements offer control within loops, allowing for early termination or skipping of iterations.

Understanding control flow in Python is crucial for writing efficient and structured programs, enabling data manipulation, and implementing complex algorithms. Careful use of loops and conditionals enhances the readability and maintainability of the code, making Python a powerful language for a wide range of programming tasks.

1. Functions and Object-Oriented Programming in Python

A. Functions in Python:

Functions are a fundamental concept in programming that allow code to be organized into reusable and modular blocks. In Python, a function is a group of related statements that perform a specific task and can be called multiple times throughout the program. Functions enhance the readability, maintainability, and efficiency of code by promoting code reuse and reducing redundancy.

- ***Function Definition:***

A function is defined using the def keyword, followed by the function name and a set of parentheses that may contain input parameters (also known as arguments). The function body is indented below the function definition and contains the code to be executed when the function is called.

```
def greet(name):
    print("Hello, " + name + "!")
```

- ***Function Call:***

To execute the code within a function, it must be called or invoked with the function name and appropriate arguments (if any).

```
greet("Nibe") # Output: Hello, Nibe!
    greet("Dita") # Output: Hello, Dita!
```

- ***Return Statement:***

Functions can also return values using the return statement. The return statement allows a function to compute a result and send it back to the caller.

```
def add(a, b):
return a + b
result = add(5, 3)

print(result) # Output: 8
```

- ***Default Arguments:***

Python functions can have default parameter values assigned. These default values are used when the function is called without providing specific arguments for those parameters.

```
def power(base, exponent=2):
return base ** exponent
print(power(3)) # Output: 9 (3^2)

print(power(2, 3)) # Output: 8 (2^3)
```

- ***Variable Number of Arguments:***

  Python functions can accept a variable number of arguments using the *args and **kwargs syntax. The *args allows passing a variable number of non-keyword arguments, while **kwargs allows passing a variable number of keyword arguments.

```
def average(*args):
return sum(args) / len(args)

print(average(10, 20, 30))
# Output: 20.0 (average of 10, 20, 30)
```

- ***Lambda Functions:***

  Lambda functions, also known as anonymous functions, are short, one-line functions defined using the lambda keyword. They are useful for simple and short operations.

```
multiply = lambda x, y: x * y

print(multiply(3, 4)) # Output: 12
```

Functions play a critical role in organizing and structuring code, making it easier to maintain and debug. They facilitate code reuse, encapsulation, and modular programming, enhancing the overall efficiency of Python programs.

B. Object-Oriented Programming (OOP) in Python:

Object-Oriented Programming (OOP) is a programming paradigm that represents data and behavior as objects. In Python, everything is an object, including integers, strings, and even functions. OOP promotes the organization of code into classes and objects, allowing for a more intuitive representation of real-world entities and their interactions.

- ***Classes and Objects:***

A class is a blueprint or a template for creating objects. It defines attributes (data members) and methods (functions) that characterize the objects of the class. An object is an instance of a class, and it can access the attributes and methods defined in the class.

- ***Class Definition:***

A class is defined using the class keyword, followed by the class name. The class body contains the attributes and methods of the class, indented below the class definition.

```
class Circle:
def __init__(self, radius):
self.radius = radius
def area(self):

    return 3.14 * self.radius * self.radius
```

- ***Object Creation:***

  To create an object of a class, the class is instantiated using the class name followed by parentheses.

```
circle1 = Circle(5)

    circle2 = Circle(7)
```

- ***Constructors and Destructors:***

  In Python, the _init_ method is a special method called a constructor. It is automatically executed when an object is created and is used to initialize the object's attributes.

```
class Student:
def _init_(self, name, age):
self.name = name
self.age = age
def display_info(self):
print("Name:", self.name)

    print("Age:", self.age)
```

- ***Inheritance:***

  Inheritance is a key feature of OOP that allows a class (subclass) to inherit attributes and methods from another class (superclass). This promotes code reuse and allows the creation of specialized classes.

```
class Car:
def __init__(self, make, model):
self.make = make
self.model = model
def display_info(self):
print("Make:", self.make)
print("Model:", self.model)
class ElectricCar(Car):
def __init__(self, make, model, battery_capacity):
super().__init__(make, model)
self.battery_capacity = battery_capacity
def display_info(self):
super().display_info()
print("Battery Capacity:", self.battery_capacity)
```

- ***Encapsulation:***

Encapsulation is the concept of hiding the implementation details of a class from external access. In Python, this is achieved by using private variables and methods, denoted by a leading double underscore ('__').

```
class BankAccount:
def __init__(self):
self.__balance = 0
def deposit(self, amount):
self.__balance += amount
def withdraw(self, amount):
if amount <= self.__balance:
self.__balance -= amount
else:
print("Insufficient balance!")
def get_balance(self):

    return self.__balance
```

- ***Polymorphism:***

Polymorphism allows objects of different classes to be treated as objects of a common superclass. This promotes code flexibility and allows for dynamic method calls.

```
class Animal:
def sound(self):
pass
class Dog(Animal):
def sound(self):
print("Bark!")
class Cat(Animal):
def sound(self):
print("Meow!")
def animal_sound(animal):
animal.sound()
dog = Dog()
cat = Cat()
animal_sound(dog) # Output: Bark!

animal_sound(cat) # Output: Meow!
```

Functions and Object-Oriented Programming (OOP) are powerful concepts in Python that enhance code organization, reuse, and efficiency. Functions allow code to be structured into reusable blocks, improving maintainability and readability. They can have default arguments, variable numbers of arguments, and even be represented as lambda functions.

Object-Oriented Programming (OOP) represents data and behavior as objects, providing a more intuitive way to model real-world entities and their interactions. Classes define the attributes and methods that characterize objects, and objects are instances of classes. OOP features include inheritance, encapsulation, constructors, destructors, and polymorphism, which contribute to code reusability, modularity, and flexibility.

Understanding functions and OOP in Python empowers programmers to design and implement efficient, scalable, and maintainable code, making Python a versatile and powerful language for a wide range of programming tasks.

Chapter 9: Essential Python Libraries for Data Science

1. NumPy for Numerical Computing

NumPy, short for "Numerical Python," is a fundamental library in Python that empowers programmers and scientists to perform efficient numerical computing and data analysis. Released in 2005, NumPy was initially developed by Travis Olliphant as an open-source project, and it has since become an integral part of the scientific Python ecosystem. With its powerful array data structure and extensive mathematical functions, NumPy has revolutionized the way numerical computations are performed in Python.

The centerpiece of NumPy is its multidimensional array object called the "ndarray" (N-dimensional array). This array data structure is the backbone of NumPy and is highly efficient for storing and manipulating large datasets. Unlike the traditional Python lists, NumPy arrays are homogeneous, meaning all elements in the array must have the same data type, leading to optimized memory consumption and faster computations.

Creating a NumPy array is straightforward. You can initialize an array from a Python list or tuple using the numpy.array() function. Alternatively, you can use specialized functions like numpy.zeros(), numpy.ones(), or numpy.random to generate arrays of specific shapes and values. This flexibility makes NumPy arrays highly versatile and suitable for a wide range of numerical applications.

NumPy provides a host of functionalities to perform various mathematical and logical operations on arrays. Broadcasting, a key feature of NumPy, allows element-wise operations between arrays of different shapes and dimensions, enabling concise and efficient code. Operations like addition, subtraction, multiplication, division, and more can be performed element-wise without the need for explicit loops, significantly improving computational performance.

One of the primary reasons for NumPy's popularity is its seamless integration with other Python libraries. Many data analysis and scientific computing libraries, such as Pandas, SciPy, and scikit-learn, rely heavily on NumPy for their core functionalities. This integration fosters a cohesive ecosystem that simplifies data manipulation, analysis, and visualization.

In addition to array operations, NumPy boasts an extensive collection of mathematical functions. These functions cover areas like linear algebra, Fourier transforms, statistical analysis, and more. Users can leverage these functions to perform complex computations with ease, significantly reducing development time and effort.

Beyond its core array and mathematical functionalities, NumPy also offers functionality for reading and writing data from/to disk, enabling seamless data storage and retrieval.

NumPy arrays can be saved in various formats, such as binary, text, or NumPy's native .npy format. This feature ensures data persistence and portability across different platforms.

Efficiency is a hallmark of NumPy, achieved through the use of low-level languages like C and Fortran for implementing core functionalities. Under the hood, NumPy's operations are executed in pre-compiled C code, making them considerably faster than equivalent Python implementations. This efficiency becomes especially crucial when dealing with large datasets or computationally intensive tasks.

Furthermore, NumPy provides tools for reshaping, slicing, and indexing arrays, making it convenient to manipulate data in different dimensions. Indexing in NumPy follows the "zero-based" convention, allowing users to access elements using integers, slices, or boolean arrays, enabling complex data extraction and filtering.

In recent years, the widespread adoption of machine learning and artificial intelligence has further boosted NumPy's popularity. Many machine learning frameworks like TensorFlow and PyTorch use NumPy-like arrays as their primary data structure for training models. This integration allows data to be seamlessly transferred between NumPy arrays and machine learning libraries, fostering a smooth workflow for researchers and data scientists.

In conclusion, NumPy has become a cornerstone of numerical computing in Python due to its powerful array data structure, extensive mathematical functions, and seamless integration with other scientific libraries. Its efficiency, versatility, and ease of use have made it a go-to choice for researchers, engineers, and data scientists alike. With the ever-growing Python ecosystem and the continuous development of new features and optimizations, NumPy's influence is likely to endure, driving innovation in the field of numerical computing for years to come.

1. Pandas for Data Manipulation and Analysis

Pandas is a widely-used Python library that has revolutionized data manipulation and analysis in the field of data science. Developed by Wes McKinney in 2008, Pandas provides powerful data structures and tools that simplify the handling and analysis of structured data. Its name is derived from "panel data," a term used in econometrics to describe multidimensional structured datasets. With its intuitive and versatile functionalities, Pandas has become an indispensable tool for data scientists, analysts, and researchers alike.

The core data structures in Pandas are the DataFrame and the Series. The DataFrame is a two-dimensional tabular data structure, akin to a spreadsheet or SQL table, with labeled axes (rows and columns). Each column in a

DataFrame can contain data of different types, such as integers, floating-point numbers, strings, or even complex objects. This flexibility allows Pandas to handle diverse datasets with ease.

The Series, on the other hand, is a one-dimensional labeled array. It can be thought of as a single column of a DataFrame. Series are particularly useful when dealing with time series data or any other data that can be represented as an ordered sequence.

Creating a DataFrame in Pandas is straightforward. Data can be loaded into a DataFrame from various sources like CSV files, Excel spreadsheets, SQL databases, or even from Python dictionaries and lists. The rich collection of I/O tools in Pandas enables users to import and export data in various formats, facilitating seamless integration with external data sources.

Pandas excels in data cleaning and transformation. It provides a wide array of methods to handle missing data, duplicate values, and outliers. The ability to reshape, pivot, and melt data makes it effortless to transform data into the desired format for analysis and visualization. With intuitive functions like drop(), fillna(), and replace(), data cleaning becomes an efficient and less cumbersome process.

Data indexing and selection in Pandas are powerful features that allow users to access specific data points quickly. Both label-based (using column and row names) and integer-based indexing are supported, providing the flexibility to extract data in various ways. Boolean indexing is another handy feature that enables users to filter data based on specific conditions, making data extraction and subsetting highly convenient.

Pandas is equipped with a wide range of data manipulation tools, including grouping and aggregating data. The groupby() function allows users to group data based on specific columns and apply various aggregate functions, such as sum, mean, max, and min, to each group. This feature is particularly useful when dealing with data that requires summarization or grouping based on certain attributes.

In addition to data manipulation, Pandas integrates seamlessly with other data analysis and visualization libraries. For instance, Pandas can be combined with Matplotlib or Seaborn to create insightful visualizations directly from DataFrames. This integration promotes a smooth workflow, from data wrangling to data exploration and presentation.

Pandas also supports time series data analysis. It provides functionality for date and time manipulation, time zone conversion, and resampling. These features are particularly useful when working with time-based data, such as financial data, IoT sensor readings, or any data that involves temporal aspects.

Furthermore, Pandas allows users to perform various statistical computations effortlessly. Descriptive statistics, correlation analysis, and linear regression are just a few examples of the statistical tools provided by Pandas. These functionalities enable users to gain deeper insights into their data and draw meaningful conclusions from the analysis.

The extensibility of Pandas is another significant advantage. Users can define custom functions and apply them to data using the apply() method. This capability allows for tailored data transformations and analysis, accommodating specific requirements of diverse datasets.

One of the crucial factors contributing to Pandas' popularity is its active community and continuous development. The library is open-source, and contributions from the community keep it updated with bug fixes, enhancements, and new features. This vibrant ecosystem ensures that Pandas remains relevant and adaptive to the evolving needs of data scientists and analysts.

In conclusion, Pandas has become the go-to library for data manipulation and analysis in Python due to its intuitive data structures, powerful data cleaning and transformation capabilities, efficient data indexing and selection, and seamless integration with other data analysis and visualization libraries. Its ability to handle structured data effectively, along with a rich set of functions for data exploration and statistical analysis, has made it an indispensable tool for anyone working with data in Python. As the data science landscape continues to evolve, Pandas is likely to remain a crucial component of the Python data science toolkit.

1. Matplotlib for Data Visualization

Matplotlib is a comprehensive data visualization library in Python that provides a wide array of tools to create visually appealing and informative plots, charts, and figures. Developed by John D. Hunter in 2003, Matplotlib has become the de facto standard for data visualization in the Python ecosystem. Its versatility, ease of use, and integration with other scientific libraries make it an essential tool for data scientists, researchers, and anyone seeking to explore and communicate insights from data visually.

At the core of Matplotlib lies the pyplot module, which provides a MATLAB-like interface for creating and customizing plots. With pyplot, users can generate line plots, scatter plots, bar charts, histograms, pie charts, and more with just a few lines of code. This high-level interface simplifies the process of creating basic visualizations and allows users to focus on the data and the insights they want to convey.

Matplotlib supports a range of output formats, enabling users to save their visualizations in various file types, such as PNG,

JPEG, PDF, and SVG. This feature ensures compatibility with different applications and allows for seamless integration of plots into documents, reports, presentations, and web applications.

The flexibility of Matplotlib enables users to fine-tune every aspect of their visualizations. From customizing colors, line styles, and marker types to setting axis labels, titles, and legends, users have complete control over the appearance and layout of their plots. This level of customization ensures that the visualizations align with the specific requirements and branding of the project.

Matplotlib's object-oriented approach provides an alternative to the pyplot interface. With the object-oriented API, users have greater control over the components of the plot. Each element of the plot, such as the figure, axes, and plot elements, is represented as an object, allowing for more complex and interactive visualizations.

Beyond the basic plot types, Matplotlib supports 3D plotting, which is particularly useful for visualizing complex datasets with an additional dimension. The mplot3d toolkit in Matplotlib provides functions for creating 3D scatter plots, surface plots, contour plots, and more, making it a valuable tool for visualizing spatial and volumetric data.

In addition to static plots, Matplotlib supports interactive visualizations using the %matplotlib notebook mode or the newer %matplotlib widget mode in Jupyter notebooks. This feature enhances the exploration of data by enabling users to zoom, pan, and interact with plots dynamically.

Matplotlib's seamless integration with Pandas, NumPy, and other scientific libraries allows users to easily visualize data stored in DataFrame and array structures. The ability to pass data directly from Pandas DataFrames to Matplotlib's plotting functions simplifies the data visualization workflow and eliminates the need for data preprocessing.

For even more advanced and specialized visualizations, Matplotlib can be extended with additional toolkits and add-ons. Seaborn, for example, is a statistical data visualization library built on top of Matplotlib. It provides a high-level interface for creating aesthetically pleasing statistical plots, and its integration with Matplotlib enhances the visualization capabilities further.

Matplotlib's active community and continuous development ensure that the library is regularly updated with bug fixes, new features, and enhancements. Feedback from the community is taken into account, making it a collaborative effort that addresses the needs of a diverse range of users.

Over the years, Matplotlib has established itself as a go-to library for data visualization, not only in Python but also in various fields such as scientific research, data analysis, and machine learning. The ability to produce publication-quality visualizations, combined with its wide-ranging support for different plot types and configurations, has contributed to its widespread adoption.

In conclusion, Matplotlib is a powerful and flexible data visualization library in Python that empowers users to create a wide range of informative and visually appealing plots and charts. Its intuitive interface, extensive customization options, and seamless integration with other scientific libraries make it an indispensable tool for exploring and communicating insights from data. As data visualization remains a critical component of data analysis and communication, Matplotlib's continued development and adaptability will ensure its relevance and utility in the ever-evolving landscape of data science.

Chapter 10: Data Wrangling and Preprocessing with Python

1. Data Cleaning Techniques

Data cleaning, also known as data cleansing or data scrubbing, is an essential step in the data preprocessing pipeline. It refers to the process of identifying and correcting errors, inconsistencies, and inaccuracies in datasets to ensure that the data is accurate, complete, and reliable for analysis and decision-making. Data cleaning techniques play a vital role in maintaining data quality and integrity, which is crucial for obtaining meaningful and trustworthy insights from the data.

The first step in data cleaning is to perform a thorough inspection of the dataset to identify potential issues. This initial exploration involves checking for missing values, duplicate entries, inconsistent formatting, outliers, and any other anomalies that may affect the quality of the data. Understanding the nature and extent of these issues is critical in selecting the appropriate data cleaning techniques to address them effectively.

Handling missing data is a common challenge in data cleaning. Missing values can arise due to various reasons, such as data entry errors, malfunctioning sensors, or participants' non-response in surveys. Several techniques can be employed to deal with missing data, including removal of rows or columns with missing values, imputation of missing values using statistical methods like mean, median, or interpolation, or using advanced machine learning algorithms to predict missing values based on other features in the dataset.

Dealing with duplicate records is another crucial aspect of data cleaning. Duplicate entries can skew analysis results and lead to erroneous conclusions. Identifying and removing duplicates can be achieved using techniques such as deduplication based on specific columns or using advanced algorithms like fuzzy matching to identify similar records with slight variations.

Inconsistent formatting is a common issue in datasets, especially when data is collected from multiple sources or entered manually. This can include variations in date formats, capitalization, spelling, or categorical values that represent the same information but are expressed differently. Standardizing the format of data is essential to maintain consistency and make data analysis more efficient. Techniques like string manipulation, regular expressions, and lookup tables can be used to achieve data standardization.

Outliers are data points that deviate significantly from the majority of the data. They can arise due to measurement errors or represent genuine extreme observations. Identifying and handling outliers is crucial as they can influence statistical analysis and machine learning models. Techniques such as statistical methods (e.g., z-score, modified z-score) or domain knowledge-based approaches can be employed to detect and deal with outliers appropriately.

Another data cleaning technique involves addressing inconsistencies between related datasets. When data is collected from different sources or at different times, there may be discrepancies that need to be resolved for accurate analysis. Data integration techniques, such as merging and joining datasets using common identifiers, can help reconcile inconsistencies and create a unified and comprehensive dataset.

Data cleaning can also involve handling data that falls outside the domain of interest or data that is no longer relevant. This may include filtering out irrelevant or outdated records to focus on the most pertinent data for analysis. Data filtering can be based on specific criteria or time intervals, depending on the context of the analysis.

Normalization and scaling are essential techniques used in data cleaning, especially when dealing with numerical data of different scales. Normalization brings all numerical variables to a common scale, often between 0 and 1, to ensure that no variable dominates the analysis due to its larger magnitude. Scaling ensures that features have a comparable range, which can improve the performance of certain machine learning algorithms and mathematical calculations.

Handling inconsistent or erroneous categorical data is critical in data cleaning. Categories with similar meanings may be represented differently, leading to confusion and inaccuracies in the analysis. Techniques like data mapping, grouping similar categories, or performing entity resolution can help resolve such issues and improve the quality of the categorical data.

Addressing data integrity problems is another important aspect of data cleaning. Data integrity ensures that data is accurate, consistent, and reliable throughout its lifecycle. This involves setting constraints and validation rules during data entry and updating processes to prevent data errors and inconsistencies.

Data cleaning is an iterative process, and it may require multiple rounds of cleansing to achieve the desired data quality. After applying various data cleaning techniques, it is crucial to validate the results to ensure that the cleaning process has not introduced new errors or distortions. Validation can involve cross-referencing the cleaned data with trusted sources, performing statistical checks, or conducting sensitivity analyses to assess the impact of data cleaning on analysis outcomes.

In conclusion, data cleaning techniques play a vital role in ensuring the accuracy, completeness, and reliability of data for meaningful analysis and decision-making.

Addressing missing values, duplicates, inconsistent formatting, outliers, and other data anomalies are key aspects of the data cleaning process. Employing appropriate data cleaning techniques and validating the results are essential to maintain data quality and integrity, leading to more accurate and reliable insights from the data. As the volume and complexity of data continue to grow, the importance of effective data cleaning techniques will only increase in the field of data science and beyond.

1. Data Transformation and Feature Scaling

Data transformation and feature scaling are crucial steps in the data preprocessing pipeline, often applied before feeding the data into machine learning algorithms. These techniques aim to modify the original data to make it more suitable for analysis and modeling, improve algorithm performance, and ensure that all features are on comparable scales. Data transformation involves converting or altering the data in various ways, while feature scaling is a specific type of data transformation that focuses on normalizing the range of feature values.

Data transformation encompasses a wide range of techniques, including converting data types, handling missing values, encoding categorical variables, and creating new features through feature engineering. One of the initial steps in data transformation is converting the data types of variables to ensure they are correctly interpreted by the analysis or modeling algorithms. For example, converting date and time strings to datetime objects or converting numerical values represented as strings to numeric data types.

Handling missing values is another critical aspect of data transformation. Missing data can arise due to various reasons, such as data collection errors or non-response in surveys.

Techniques like imputation, where missing values are replaced with estimated values based on other data points, are commonly used to address missing data. Imputation methods can be based on statistical measures such as mean, median, or mode, or more advanced techniques like regression models or k-nearest neighbors.

Encoding categorical variables is essential when dealing with non-numeric data, as most machine learning algorithms require numerical inputs. Categorical data can be one-hot encoded, where each category is represented by a binary variable, or label encoded, where categories are mapped to integer values. Care must be taken with one-hot encoding to avoid the "dummy variable trap," where highly correlated binary variables lead to multicollinearity in regression models.

Feature engineering is a powerful data transformation technique that involves creating new features from existing ones to improve model performance. This process can include deriving time-based features from date-time variables, extracting text features like word counts or sentiment scores, or combining multiple features to create interaction terms. Feature engineering allows the algorithm to capture more complex patterns and relationships in the data, leading to more accurate and robust models.

Feature scaling is a specific type of data transformation that focuses on bringing all features to a similar scale. Many machine learning algorithms use distance-based calculations, and features with larger scales can dominate the model's learning process. By scaling the features to a common range, all features contribute equally to the model, preventing any one feature from having a disproportionate impact.

One of the most common methods of feature scaling is standardization, also known as z-score normalization. In standardization, each feature is transformed to have a mean of 0 and a standard deviation of 1. This process centers the data around 0 and scales it according to the spread of the data, making it suitable for algorithms that assume Gaussian distributions or require data on a similar scale.

Another popular feature scaling technique is min-max scaling, where the values of each feature are scaled to a specific range, typically between 0 and 1. This method is particularly useful when the algorithm or model requires data within a bounded range. Min-max scaling is less affected by outliers compared to standardization, as it preserves the relative relationships between the data points.

Robust scaling is a variant of feature scaling that is less sensitive to outliers. It uses the median and interquartile range (IQR) to scale the data, making it suitable for data with extreme values or heavy-tailed distributions. By using robust scaling, the impact of outliers on the scaled data is minimized, leading to more stable and accurate modeling results.

Normalization is another feature scaling technique that scales each data point to a unit norm. This process is often used when the direction of the data points is more important than their magnitude. Normalization is commonly used in clustering algorithms, such as k-means, where the distance between data points determines their similarity.

Principal Component Analysis (PCA) is an advanced data transformation technique that involves reducing the dimensionality of the data while preserving as much of the original variance as possible. PCA transforms the original features into a new set of uncorrelated features, called principal components, which are ordered by the amount of variance they capture. By retaining only the most significant principal components, the data can be represented in a lower-dimensional space, reducing computational complexity and mitigating the curse of dimensionality.

In conclusion, data transformation and feature scaling are essential steps in the data preprocessing pipeline for data analysis and machine learning. Data transformation involves converting data types, handling missing values, encoding categorical variables, and feature engineering to prepare the data for modeling. Feature scaling, on the other hand, focuses on normalizing the range of feature values to ensure that all features contribute equally to the learning process. These techniques play a critical role in improving algorithm performance, ensuring numerical stability, and facilitating the extraction of meaningful insights from data. By applying appropriate data transformation and feature scaling methods, data scientists and analysts can enhance the quality and efficiency of their data analysis and modeling tasks.

1. Handling Missing Data

Handling missing data is a critical aspect of data science and data analysis. Missing data refers to the absence of values in a dataset, which can occur for various reasons, such as data collection errors, non-response in surveys, or equipment malfunctions. Dealing with missing data is essential because the presence of missing values can lead to biased results, inaccurate conclusions, and hinder the performance of machine learning algorithms. Data scientists employ various techniques to handle missing data effectively, such as deletion, imputation, and advanced methods that take into account the underlying patterns and relationships in the data.

The first step in handling missing data is to identify and quantify the extent of missingness in the dataset. Data scientists typically perform a missing data analysis to determine the percentage of missing values for each variable.

This analysis helps in understanding the patterns of missingness and allows them to make informed decisions about the appropriate handling techniques. Additionally, it is essential to differentiate between different types of missing data, such as missing completely at random (MCAR), missing at random (MAR), and missing not at random (MNAR), as the missingness mechanism can influence the choice of handling methods.

The simplest approach to handling missing data is deletion, where records or variables with missing values are removed from the dataset. Listwise deletion, also known as complete-case analysis, involves removing entire rows containing at least one missing value. Pairwise deletion, on the other hand, involves retaining rows for analysis when the specific variables of interest have complete data. While deletion is straightforward, it can lead to loss of information and reduce the representativeness of the dataset, especially if missing data patterns are not random.

Imputation is another widely used technique for handling missing data, where missing values are replaced with estimated values. Imputation helps retain the complete dataset and allows the use of all available information for analysis. There are several imputation methods available, including mean imputation, median imputation, mode imputation, and hot-deck imputation. Mean and median imputation replace missing values with the mean or median of the non-missing values in the respective variable. Mode imputation, on the other hand, replaces missing values with the most frequent value of the variable. Hot-deck imputation involves matching cases with missing values to similar cases with complete data based on certain attributes.

More sophisticated imputation methods involve using machine learning algorithms or statistical models to estimate missing values based on the relationships between variables. Regression imputation uses regression models to predict missing values based on other variables in the dataset. Multiple imputation, a probabilistic approach, generates several imputed datasets, and the analysis is performed on each dataset, with the results combined to obtain more robust estimates and standard errors.

Another method for handling missing data is using interpolation techniques, where missing values are estimated based on the trend or pattern of the surrounding data points. Time series data, for instance, can be interpolated using techniques like linear interpolation, cubic interpolation, or seasonal decomposition of time series (STL) imputation.

Advanced techniques for handling missing data include the use of clustering algorithms to group similar data points and impute missing values based on the attributes of the clusters. Bayesian imputation, which leverages the principles of Bayesian statistics, provides a probabilistic framework for imputing missing data, capturing uncertainty in the imputed values.

Domain-specific knowledge and expertise also play a vital role in handling missing data. Data scientists and domain experts often use their understanding of the data and the context in which it was collected to impute missing values in a meaningful and accurate manner. For instance, in healthcare data, missing laboratory test results might be imputed based on a patient's medical history, diagnosis, and other relevant factors.

While handling missing data, it is crucial to assess the impact of the chosen imputation method on the analysis results. Sensitivity analysis, where multiple imputation methods are compared and their effects on the analysis are evaluated, can help gauge the robustness of the conclusions drawn from the imputed data.

It is essential to be cautious when handling missing data to avoid introducing biases or inaccuracies in the analysis. Missing data imputation should be based on sound statistical principles and should not introduce additional patterns or distort the underlying distribution of the data. Properly addressing missing data can lead to more reliable and accurate results, contributing to better decision-making and more informed insights from the data.

In conclusion, handling missing data is a crucial aspect of data science and data analysis. Missing data can occur for various reasons and can impact the accuracy and reliability of analysis results. Data scientists employ a range of techniques, such as deletion, imputation, interpolation, and advanced methods, to handle missing data effectively. The choice of the appropriate method depends on the characteristics of the missing data, the analysis goals, and the context in which the data was collected. By using careful and principled approaches to handle missing data, data scientists can ensure the integrity and quality of their analysis results, leading to more robust and meaningful insights from the data.

Chapter 11: Data Visualization Techniques with Matplotlib and Seaborn

1. Creating Basic Plots: Line, Bar, and Scatter

Creating basic plots, such as line plots, bar charts, and scatter plots, is a fundamental skill in data science and data visualization. These types of plots are versatile and widely used to visualize various types of data and relationships between variables. Data scientists use plotting libraries, such as Matplotlib in Python, to generate these basic plots and gain insights into the data distribution, trends, and patterns.

Line plots are a common type of plot used to visualize the relationship between two variables that are both continuous. The x-axis typically represents the independent variable, while the y-axis represents the dependent variable. Line plots are ideal for displaying trends, patterns, and changes over time or any continuous scale. For example, line plots are often used to visualize stock market trends, temperature variations, or sales trends over time. In Matplotlib, creating a line plot is straightforward. The plt.plot() function is used to plot the data, and additional customization can be applied to the plot, such as adding labels, titles, and legends, to enhance its readability and interpretability.

Bar charts are widely used for visualizing categorical data or discrete variables. In a bar chart, each category or level of the variable is represented by a bar, and the height of the bar corresponds to the frequency or count of that category. Bar charts are effective for comparing different categories and identifying the most prevalent or least prevalent categories in the data. For example, a bar chart can be used to visualize the distribution of product sales across different regions or the number of students in various grade levels. In Matplotlib, creating a bar chart is achieved using the plt.bar() function. Users can customize the appearance of the bars, add labels, and modify the color scheme to create visually appealing and informative bar charts.

Scatter plots are used to visualize the relationship between two continuous variables. Each data point is represented as a point on the plot, with the x-coordinate corresponding to one variable and the y-coordinate corresponding to the other variable. Scatter plots are helpful in identifying patterns such as correlation, clusters, or outliers in the data. For example, a scatter plot can be used to visualize the relationship between a student's study time and their exam scores or to explore the correlation between two financial indicators. In Matplotlib, scatter plots can be created using the plt.scatter() function. Additional customization options, such as adding labels and colors based on a third variable, allow for richer visualizations and insights.

In data science, creating these basic plots is often the first step in exploring and understanding the data. Line plots help identify trends and temporal patterns, bar charts help understand the distribution of categorical variables, and scatter plots aid in discovering relationships and potential correlations between continuous variables.

When creating line plots, data scientists must ensure that the data is appropriately sorted to visualize trends accurately. Additionally, smoothing techniques, such as moving averages or polynomial fitting, can be applied to reduce noise in the data and highlight underlying patterns.

Bar charts benefit from proper selection of the categorical variable and the order in which the bars are displayed. Labeling the bars and using horizontal bar charts for long category names can improve the clarity of the visualization.

For scatter plots, data scientists should be cautious about the presence of outliers or influential data points that may distort the apparent relationships. Regression lines or other fitting methods can be added to the scatter plot to visualize the overall trend between the variables.

In addition to creating individual basic plots, data scientists often combine multiple plots into a single visualization to gain a comprehensive view of the data. Subplots can be used to display related line plots, bar charts, or scatter plots side by side for comparison. Combining different types of plots in a single visualization can enhance the storytelling capability and provide a more holistic understanding of the data.

Data scientists also use interactive plotting libraries, such as Plotly and Bokeh, to create dynamic and interactive visualizations. Interactive plots allow users to explore the data by zooming, panning, and hovering over data points for additional information. These interactive features enhance data exploration and facilitate deeper insights into the data.

In conclusion, creating basic plots, including line plots, bar charts, and scatter plots, is a fundamental skill in data science and data visualization. These types of plots help data scientists explore data, identify patterns, and communicate insights effectively. Matplotlib provides a powerful and flexible tool for generating these basic plots in Python, while interactive plotting libraries like Plotly and Bokeh offer additional capabilities for dynamic and interactive data visualization. By mastering the art of creating basic plots, data scientists can better understand the data, uncover valuable patterns, and make informed decisions based on data-driven insights.

1. Customizing Plots for Effective Visualization

Customizing plots for effective visualization is a crucial aspect of data science and data analysis.

While creating basic plots like line plots, bar charts, and scatter plots provides a foundation for data exploration, customizing plots allows data scientists to enhance the visual clarity, highlight important insights, and improve the overall impact of the visualizations. By carefully selecting colors, labels, titles, axes, legends, and other visual elements, data scientists can create compelling and informative visualizations that effectively communicate their findings to stakeholders and decision-makers.

One of the key considerations in customizing plots is selecting appropriate colors and color schemes. Colors can be used to differentiate categories or highlight specific data points. Data scientists should be mindful of color choices, especially for categorical variables in bar charts and pie charts, to ensure that each category is easily distinguishable. Colors can also be used to represent a third variable in scatter plots, allowing for more complex visualizations that reveal multivariate relationships. It is essential to consider color blindness and avoid using color combinations that might be difficult for color-blind individuals to interpret. Plotting libraries, such as Matplotlib, provide predefined color palettes and allow custom color selection to suit the specific requirements of the data and the visualization.

Labels and titles play a crucial role in conveying the meaning and context of the visualization. Clear and descriptive labels for the x-axis, y-axis, and plot title help viewers understand what the plot represents without the need for additional explanations. In bar charts and line plots, data scientists can include data labels directly on the bars or data points to provide exact values and improve the interpretability of the plot. When plotting time series data, meaningful date and time labels on the x-axis aid in understanding temporal patterns and trends. Properly labeled axes and titles ensure that the visualizations are self-contained and easily understandable.

Adding annotations and textual explanations to the plot can further enhance its interpretability. Annotations can be used to highlight specific data points, outliers, or key events in the data. Data scientists can also include informative text boxes or callouts to provide additional context or insights about the data. Annotations and explanatory text help guide viewers' attention to essential aspects of the visualization and enhance the storytelling aspect of the data analysis.

Legends are essential when plotting multiple data series or when representing different categories in the same plot. Legends help viewers understand the meaning of different colors, line styles, or markers used in the plot. Customizing the legend's position, size, and formatting can help improve the readability of the visualization, especially when dealing with a large number of data series. Legends should be clear and concise, avoiding clutter and confusion in the plot.

The choice of plot type and visualization layout also contributes to the effectiveness of the visualization. Depending on the data and the message to be conveyed, data scientists can choose from various types of plots, such as histograms, box plots, area plots, and heatmaps, among others. Choosing the right plot type ensures that the data is presented in a manner that best highlights its characteristics and relationships. Additionally, creating subplots or small multiples, where multiple plots are displayed side by side, allows for easy comparison and facilitates the exploration of multiple aspects of the data simultaneously.

Plot aesthetics, such as grid lines, tick marks, and background color, can be customized to improve the readability of the plot. Removing unnecessary grid lines or using a light-colored background can reduce visual clutter and draw attention to the data points or bars. Appropriate tick marks on the axes help in understanding the scale of the data and ensure that the visual representation accurately reflects the underlying data values.

Plot size and aspect ratio are important considerations, especially when preparing visualizations for reports, presentations, or publications. Data scientists should select an appropriate plot size that balances the need for detail and the desire to make efficient use of space. The aspect ratio of the plot can be adjusted to avoid distortion and maintain the proportions of the data. Customizing plot size and aspect ratio ensures that the visualizations are visually appealing and easily interpretable by the audience.

In addition to static visualizations, data scientists can use interactive plotting libraries, such as Plotly and Bokeh, to create dynamic and interactive visualizations. Interactive features, such as zooming, panning, tooltips, and interactive legends, enable users to explore the data in more depth. Interactive visualizations are especially useful when presenting complex data or when the audience needs to interact with the data to gain deeper insights.

In conclusion, customizing plots for effective visualization is a vital skill in data science and data analysis. By carefully selecting colors, labels, titles, annotations, legends, and other visual elements, data scientists can create compelling and informative visualizations that effectively communicate their findings to stakeholders and decision-makers. Properly customized plots improve the interpretability of the data, highlight important insights, and enhance the storytelling aspect of the data analysis. Whether using basic plots or advanced interactive visualizations, customization ensures that the visual representations of the data are visually appealing, informative, and impactful.

1. Advanced Visualization: Heatmaps, Subplots, and 3D Plots

Advanced visualization techniques, such as heatmaps, subplots, and 3D plots, play a crucial role in data science and data analysis. These techniques go beyond basic plots and provide data scientists with more sophisticated ways to explore and present complex data patterns, relationships, and trends. By leveraging these advanced visualization tools, data scientists can gain deeper insights into their data and effectively communicate their findings to stakeholders.

Heatmaps are powerful visualizations that display data as a grid of colors, where each cell's color represents the value of a variable or the relationship between two variables. Heatmaps are commonly used to visualize correlation matrices, where the colors indicate the strength and direction of correlations between variables. Darker colors represent strong positive correlations, lighter colors indicate weak correlations or no correlation, and negative correlations are often represented by distinct colors. Heatmaps help identify clusters of positively or negatively correlated variables and provide a visual summary of the relationships within the dataset. In Python, libraries such as Seaborn and Matplotlib offer straightforward functions for creating heatmaps and customizing color schemes to suit the specific requirements of the data.

Subplots, also known as small multiples, are a technique used to display multiple plots or visualizations side by side in a single figure. Subplots are useful when data scientists want to compare different aspects of the data or showcase variations across different subsets of the data. For example, a data scientist might create a line plot and a scatter plot side by side to compare the trends and relationships between two variables. Subplots allow for more efficient use of space and help avoid clutter, making it easier for viewers to compare and contrast different visualizations. In Python, libraries like Matplotlib provide functions to create subplots and customize their layout, including the number of rows and columns in the grid and the spacing between the subplots.

3D plots are a valuable tool for visualizing data with three dimensions. In contrast to 2D plots, which display data on two axes, 3D plots add an additional dimension through the depth axis. 3D plots are commonly used in scientific fields to visualize three-dimensional data points or surfaces. For example, in materials science, 3D plots are used to visualize crystal structures or molecular geometries. In data science, 3D scatter plots allow for the exploration of relationships between three variables simultaneously. Libraries such as Matplotlib and Plotly provide functions for creating 3D plots and customizing their appearance, such as adjusting the viewing angle or adding color scales to represent additional variables.

Customization is an important aspect of advanced visualization techniques. Data scientists can customize heatmaps by selecting color palettes, changing the scale of the color map, and adding annotations to provide more context to the heatmap. For subplots, customization involves adjusting the size and aspect ratio of individual plots, as well as setting the layout of the subplots to optimize the visual representation. For 3D plots, data scientists can customize the viewing angle, axis labels, and plot size to ensure the most informative representation of the data.

When working with large datasets or high-dimensional data, advanced visualization techniques can help reveal patterns and structures that may be challenging to identify in basic plots. For example, in high-dimensional data, heatmaps can be used to visualize hierarchical clustering or distance matrices to identify groups or clusters of similar data points. Subplots can be used to display different dimensions of the data in separate plots, enabling data scientists to explore relationships and trends between variables in a more focused manner. 3D plots can help in visualizing complex relationships between three variables, providing a more comprehensive view of the data.

When using advanced visualization techniques, data scientists should be mindful of data preprocessing and appropriate scaling. For example, when creating heatmaps, data should be standardized or normalized to ensure that variables with different scales do not dominate the visualization. For 3D plots, data scaling and normalization are crucial to ensure that the three dimensions are visually comparable and interpretable. Additionally, data scientists should consider the context and purpose of the visualization to select the most appropriate technique and ensure that the visualizations effectively communicate the intended message to the audience.

In conclusion, advanced visualization techniques, including heatmaps, subplots, and 3D plots, are powerful tools in data science and data analysis. These techniques provide data scientists with more sophisticated ways to explore and present complex data patterns, relationships, and trends. Customization is key to ensuring that the visualizations effectively communicate insights from the data and align with the specific goals of the analysis. By leveraging these advanced visualization tools, data scientists can gain deeper insights into their data and enhance the communication of their findings to stakeholders and decision-makers.

Unit IV: Machine Learning Basics

Machine learning is a subfield of artificial intelligence that focuses on developing algorithms and statistical models that enable computers to learn from data and make predictions or decisions without being explicitly programmed for each specific task. The core idea behind machine learning is to create models that can generalize patterns from the data they are exposed to and use this knowledge to make accurate predictions or decisions on new, unseen data. Machine learning is widely used in various industries, including finance, healthcare, marketing, and robotics, and has revolutionized the way we approach problem-solving and decision-making.

The foundation of machine learning lies in the data. A typical machine learning workflow starts with data collection and preprocessing. The data collected should be relevant to the problem at hand and representative of the real-world scenarios it aims to address. Data preprocessing involves cleaning, transforming, and normalizing the data to remove noise, handle missing values, and ensure that it is in a suitable format for the learning algorithms. High-quality and properly preprocessed data form the backbone of successful machine learning models.

Once the data is ready, the next step is to split it into two sets: the training set and the testing set. The training set is used to train the machine learning model, while the testing set is used to evaluate the model's performance on new, unseen data. The goal of machine learning is to create models that can generalize well from the training data to make accurate predictions or decisions on the testing data.

Supervised learning and unsupervised learning are the two main categories of machine learning algorithms. In supervised learning, the model is trained on a labeled dataset, where each data point is associated with a corresponding target or output value. The model learns to map input features to the correct output labels during training. Common supervised learning tasks include classification, where the model predicts a categorical label, and regression, where the model predicts a continuous value.

Unsupervised learning, on the other hand, deals with unlabeled data, and the model is tasked with finding patterns and structures in the data without explicit guidance. Clustering and dimensionality reduction are typical unsupervised learning tasks. Clustering involves grouping similar data points together, while dimensionality reduction aims to reduce the number of input features while preserving the essential information.

Another important category of machine learning is reinforcement learning, where an agent learns to make decisions by interacting with an environment. The agent takes actions, receives feedback in the form of rewards or penalties, and uses this feedback to improve its decision-making over time. Reinforcement learning is particularly useful in settings where there is no labeled training data available and the agent must learn from trial and error.

To train a machine learning model, various algorithms are used, such as decision trees, support vector machines, k-nearest neighbors, neural networks, and many more. Each algorithm has its strengths and weaknesses, and the choice of algorithm depends on the nature of the data, the complexity of the problem, and the performance requirements.

After training the model, it is essential to evaluate its performance to assess how well it generalizes to new data. Evaluation metrics vary based on the type of machine learning task. For classification tasks, metrics like accuracy, precision, recall, and F1 score are commonly used. In regression tasks, metrics such as mean squared error (MSE) and mean absolute error (MAE) are often employed.

The final step in the machine learning workflow is deploying the trained model to make predictions on new, real-world data. The model's performance is continuously monitored and updated as new data becomes available to ensure that it remains accurate and effective over time.

Machine learning has opened up a world of possibilities, from automating routine tasks to enabling groundbreaking applications like self-driving cars and personalized medicine. However, it is essential to approach machine learning with caution and ethics, as the decisions made by machine learning models can have significant real-world implications. Transparency, fairness, and accountability are essential considerations in the development and deployment of machine learning systems.

In conclusion, machine learning is a transformative field of artificial intelligence that enables computers to learn from data and make predictions or decisions without explicit programming. It involves data collection, preprocessing, model training, evaluation, and deployment. Supervised learning, unsupervised learning, and reinforcement learning are the main categories of machine learning algorithms. Data quality and appropriate algorithm selection are critical to the success of machine learning projects. As the field continues to advance, machine learning will continue to revolutionize industries and drive innovation in various domains.

Chapter 12: Introduction to Machine Learning

1. Supervised, Unsupervised, and Reinforcement Learning

Supervised Learning:

Supervised learning is a fundamental category of machine learning algorithms where the model is trained on a labeled dataset, meaning that each data point is associated with a corresponding target or output value. The goal of supervised learning is to learn a mapping from input features to the correct output labels or target values. During the training process, the model is exposed to a set of input-output pairs and adjusts its internal parameters to minimize the discrepancy between its predictions and the true target values.

There are two main types of supervised learning tasks: classification and regression. In classification, the output variable is categorical, and the model's task is to assign input data points to one of the predefined classes or categories. For instance, a classification model can be trained to distinguish between images of cats and dogs or predict whether an email is spam or not.

In regression, the output variable is continuous, and the model's objective is to predict a numeric value based on the input features. For example, a regression model can be trained to predict housing prices based on factors like location, size, and number of rooms.

Supervised learning algorithms use various techniques, such as decision trees, support vector machines (SVM), k-nearest neighbors (KNN), and neural networks, to learn the relationships between input features and output labels. The choice of algorithm depends on the nature of the data, the complexity of the problem, and the performance requirements.

Unsupervised Learning:

In contrast to supervised learning, unsupervised learning deals with unlabeled data, where the model is not provided with corresponding target values. The objective of unsupervised learning is to find patterns, structures, or relationships within the data without any explicit guidance. Unsupervised learning is particularly useful when there is no clear notion of output labels or when the goal is to explore the underlying structure of the data.

Clustering and dimensionality reduction are two common types of unsupervised learning tasks. In clustering, the model groups similar data points together based on their similarity in feature space. The goal is to identify natural groupings or clusters in the data. For example, a clustering algorithm can be used to segment customers into distinct groups based on their purchasing behavior.

Dimensionality reduction aims to reduce the number of input features while preserving the essential information in the data. High-dimensional data can be challenging to visualize and analyze, and dimensionality reduction techniques, such as principal component analysis (PCA) or t-distributed stochastic neighbor embedding (t-SNE), help transform the data into a lower-dimensional space while retaining its structure.

Unsupervised learning algorithms leverage various mathematical and statistical techniques, such as k-means clustering, hierarchical clustering, and autoencoders, to explore the data's inherent structure and relationships. Unsupervised learning is valuable for data exploration, anomaly detection, and feature extraction.

Reinforcement Learning:

Reinforcement learning is a distinct type of machine learning that involves an agent learning to make decisions by interacting with an environment. The agent takes actions in the environment, receives feedback in the form of rewards or penalties, and uses this feedback to improve its decision-making strategy over time. The objective of reinforcement learning is to maximize the cumulative reward or long-term return that the agent receives from the environment.

The agent follows a trial-and-error approach, exploring different actions and learning from the outcomes. Reinforcement learning is well-suited for sequential decision-making tasks and scenarios where the optimal action is not immediately apparent. Examples of reinforcement learning applications include game playing, robotic control, and autonomous vehicle navigation.

The core components of reinforcement learning include the agent, the environment, actions, states, rewards, and a policy. The agent takes actions based on its current policy, which is the strategy for selecting actions in different states. The environment responds to the agent's actions, transitioning to new states and providing rewards or penalties based on the agent's decisions.

The agent learns from its interactions with the environment using various algorithms, such as Q-learning, Deep Q-Networks (DQNs), and policy gradients. Reinforcement learning can be challenging as the agent must strike a balance between exploration and exploitation to learn an effective policy without getting stuck in suboptimal actions.

Hybrid Learning Approaches:

In practice, many real-world problems may require a combination of supervised, unsupervised, and reinforcement learning techniques. For example, semi-supervised learning uses both labeled and unlabeled data to improve the performance of a model, especially when labeled data is scarce. Transfer learning involves leveraging knowledge learned from one task or domain to improve performance on a different but related task or domain.

Additionally, generative adversarial networks (GANs) combine supervised and unsupervised learning by pitting two neural networks against each other—the generator and the discriminator—to generate new data samples that resemble the training data. GANs have demonstrated remarkable capabilities in generating realistic images, audio, and other data types.

In conclusion, supervised learning, unsupervised learning, and reinforcement learning are the three main categories of machine learning algorithms, each serving different purposes and addressing various types of problems. Supervised learning is used for tasks with labeled data, such as classification and regression. Unsupervised learning explores patterns and structures in unlabeled data through clustering and dimensionality reduction. Reinforcement learning enables agents to learn from interaction with an environment and make sequential decisions to maximize rewards. Furthermore, hybrid learning approaches and innovative techniques continually push the boundaries of machine learning, contributing to groundbreaking applications and advancements in artificial intelligence.

1. Overfitting, Underfitting, and Bias-Variance Tradeoff

Overfitting, underfitting, and the bias-variance tradeoff are critical concepts in machine learning that relate to the performance and generalization ability of a model. As models are trained on data, they may encounter different issues that impact their ability to make accurate predictions on new, unseen data. Understanding these concepts is essential for data scientists to develop effective machine learning models and avoid common pitfalls.

Overfitting occurs when a machine learning model performs exceedingly well on the training data but fails to generalize to new, unseen data.

In other words, the model becomes too specific to the training data and captures noise or random fluctuations present in the data, rather than the underlying patterns. Overfitting can be thought of as memorization of the training data, rather than learning from it. As a result, an overfitted model exhibits low bias (it fits the training data well) but high variance (it does not generalize well to new data).

There are several reasons why overfitting can occur. One common reason is when the model is too complex, having too many parameters or features relative to the size of the training data. This allows the model to capture even the smallest variations in the data, leading to overfitting. Another reason is when the training data is noisy or contains outliers, causing the model to fit to these irregularities.

To address overfitting, several techniques can be employed. One approach is to use regularization, which adds a penalty term to the model's loss function to discourage complex models. This helps prevent the model from fitting the noise in the data and encourages it to focus on the most relevant features. Another technique is cross-validation, where the data is split into multiple subsets, and the model is trained on different combinations of these subsets. This allows for a more robust evaluation of the model's performance on different subsets of the data, helping to detect overfitting.

On the other hand, underfitting occurs when a machine learning model is too simplistic to capture the underlying patterns in the data. An underfitted model has high bias, meaning it does not perform well even on the training data, as it fails to capture the underlying relationships. Underfitting can happen for various reasons, such as using an overly simple model that cannot represent the complexity of the data or when the model lacks sufficient training data to learn meaningful patterns.

An underfitted model may result from selecting a linear model for data with a nonlinear relationship or using a low-degree polynomial when a higher degree is necessary. Underfitting can be identified when the model's performance is poor both on the training data and on new data.

To address underfitting, data scientists can use more complex models that have the capacity to learn from the data effectively. For instance, if a linear model is underfitting the data, using a more sophisticated model like a decision tree or a neural network may improve performance. Additionally, increasing the amount of training data can also help an underfitted model learn more accurate patterns.

The bias-variance tradeoff is a fundamental concept in machine learning that connects overfitting and underfitting. It is the balance between two types of errors that models can make: bias error and variance error.

Bias error refers to the error introduced by the model's assumptions about the data. A high-bias model is overly simplistic and may fail to capture the true underlying relationships in the data. It results in underfitting and performs poorly both on the training data and new data. On the other hand, a low-bias model has more flexibility and can fit the training data well, but it may capture noise and fluctuations in the data, leading to overfitting and poor performance on new data.

Variance error, on the other hand, refers to the model's sensitivity to small changes in the training data. A high-variance model is too sensitive to the training data and captures noise, resulting in overfitting. Such a model may perform well on the training data but poorly on new data. In contrast, a low-variance model is more robust to small changes in the data and generalizes better to new data, but it may not fit the training data well, resulting in underfitting.

The goal of machine learning is to find the right balance between bias and variance to achieve a model that generalizes well to new, unseen data. This is known as the bias-variance tradeoff. Achieving a good bias-variance tradeoff involves selecting an appropriate model complexity and optimizing hyperparameters.

Regularization techniques, as mentioned earlier, help control model complexity and reduce variance, striking a balance between overfitting and underfitting. Cross-validation is also a useful tool for evaluating different models and tuning hyperparameters to achieve the best tradeoff.

In conclusion, overfitting, underfitting, and the bias-variance tradeoff are essential concepts in machine learning. Overfitting occurs when a model memorizes the training data but fails to generalize to new data, while underfitting occurs when a model is too simplistic to capture the underlying patterns.

The bias-variance tradeoff represents the balance between bias error (due to model simplicity) and variance error (due to model sensitivity to data fluctuations). Data scientists need to understand these concepts to develop effective machine learning models that generalize well to new data and avoid common pitfalls associated with overfitting and underfitting. Proper model selection, regularization, and hyperparameter tuning are crucial to achieving the right balance between bias and variance and achieving high-performing machine learning models.

1. Cross-Validation and Model Selection

Cross-validation and model selection are fundamental techniques in machine learning that help data scientists assess the performance of their models and choose the best model for a given task. These techniques are critical for building robust and accurate machine learning models and preventing common pitfalls, such as overfitting and underfitting.

Cross-validation is a resampling technique used to evaluate the performance of a machine learning model on a limited dataset. It involves dividing the data into multiple subsets, or "folds," and iteratively training the model on different combinations of these folds. The model's performance is then evaluated on the remaining data that was not used during training. Cross-validation provides a more robust estimate of a model's performance compared to traditional train-test splits because it uses all the data for training and testing. It helps in reducing the bias introduced by a single train-test split and gives a better indication of how the model will generalize to new, unseen data.

One of the most common cross-validation techniques is k-fold cross-validation. In k-fold cross-validation, the data is divided into k subsets of approximately equal size. The model is trained on k-1 subsets (folds) and evaluated on the remaining fold. This process is repeated k times, with each fold used as the test set exactly once. The performance metrics from each fold are then averaged to obtain the final evaluation of the model's performance.

Cross-validation can help identify issues like overfitting and underfitting. If a model performs well on the training data but poorly on the test data, it may be overfitting. On the other hand, if the model performs poorly on both the training and test data, it may be underfitting. By analyzing the cross-validation results, data scientists can adjust the model's complexity, such as using regularization or feature selection, to improve its generalization ability.

Model selection is the process of choosing the best model among a set of candidate models for a given machine learning task. It involves comparing the performance of different models using evaluation metrics such as accuracy, precision, recall, F1 score, or mean squared error (MSE). Model selection is crucial because selecting the right model can significantly impact the performance of the machine learning system.

One of the common practices in model selection is to use cross-validation as a means to assess each candidate model's performance. Data scientists train multiple models with different hyperparameters, architectures, or algorithms and evaluate each model using k-fold cross-validation. By comparing the average performance of each model across the k folds, they can identify the model that performs the best on the data and has the most robust performance.

When selecting a model, it is essential to consider the tradeoff between model complexity and performance. A more complex model with a larger number of parameters may perform well on the training data (low bias) but could overfit the data and perform poorly on new, unseen data (high variance). On the other hand, a simpler model with fewer parameters may have lower variance but could underfit the data and not capture the underlying patterns (high bias). The goal is to find the right balance between bias and variance to achieve the best generalization performance.

In addition to evaluating a model's performance using cross-validation, other factors can also guide model selection. These include the interpretability of the model, computational resources required for training and inference, and domain-specific considerations. For example, in medical applications, interpretability and explainability of the model are critical for gaining the trust of medical professionals.

Ensemble methods are another powerful approach for model selection. Ensemble methods combine the predictions of multiple models to improve overall performance.

Examples of ensemble methods include bagging, where multiple models are trained independently on different subsets of the data and their predictions are averaged, and boosting, where weak learners are iteratively trained, and their predictions are combined to form a stronger model. Ensemble methods can help mitigate the risk of overfitting and improve the robustness of the final model.

Hyperparameter tuning is another important aspect of model selection. Hyperparameters are parameters that are not learned from the data during training, such as learning rate, regularization strength, and the number of layers in a neural network. The selection of appropriate hyperparameter values significantly impacts a model's performance. Grid search and random search are commonly used techniques for hyperparameter tuning, where different combinations of hyperparameter values are evaluated using cross-validation to find the optimal configuration.

Cross-validation allows data scientists to evaluate a model's performance on different subsets of the data and provides a more robust estimate of its generalization ability. Model selection involves comparing the performance of different models using cross-validation and selecting the best-performing model for the given task. It requires careful consideration of the tradeoff between model complexity and performance, as well as the interpretability and computational requirements of the models. Ensemble methods and hyperparameter tuning can further improve model selection and lead to more accurate and robust machine learning models. By effectively applying cross-validation and model selection, data scientists can build reliable and high-performing machine learning systems that meet the demands of various real-world applications.

Chapter 13: Supervised Learning: Regression and Classification

1. Linear Regression and Polynomial Regression

Linear regression and polynomial regression are two widely used supervised learning algorithms in machine learning. They both fall under the category of regression, where the goal is to predict a continuous output variable based on input features. These regression techniques are fundamental in various fields, such as economics, finance, engineering, and social sciences, for modeling and predicting numerical values.

Linear regression is a simple yet powerful method that assumes a linear relationship between the input features and the output variable. In linear regression, the goal is to find the best-fitting straight line through the data points, which minimizes the vertical distance (residuals) between the observed values and the predicted values. The line's equation is in the form of y = mx + b, where y represents the predicted output, x is the input feature, m is the slope of the line, and b is the y-intercept.

The slope (m) represents the change in the output variable (y) for a one-unit change in the input feature (x). The y-intercept (b) is the value of the output variable when the input feature is zero. The process of finding the best-fitting line involves estimating the values of m and b from the training data.

To find the optimal values of m and b, linear regression uses a cost function that measures the difference between the predicted values and the actual values in the training data. The most common cost function used in linear regression is the mean squared error (MSE), which calculates the average squared difference between the predicted and actual values. The goal is to minimize the MSE, which leads to the best-fitting line.

Once the optimal values of m and b are determined, the linear regression model can be used to make predictions on new data by substituting the input features into the line's equation. Linear regression is a straightforward and interpretable algorithm, making it a popular choice for simple regression tasks.

However, linear regression's assumption of a linear relationship may not hold for all datasets. In cases where the relationship between the input features and the output variable is nonlinear, polynomial regression can be a more suitable approach.

Polynomial regression is an extension of linear regression that models nonlinear relationships between the input features and the output variable. In polynomial regression, the relationship between the input feature (x) and the output variable (y) is approximated using a polynomial function of degree n. The polynomial equation is in the form of y = b0 + b1x + b2x^2 + ... + bnx^n, where n is the degree of the polynomial and bi's are the coefficients to be estimated from the training data.

By using higher-degree polynomials, polynomial regression can capture more complex relationships between the input features and the output variable. For example, a second-degree polynomial (n=2) can model a quadratic relationship, while a third-degree polynomial (n=3) can model a cubic relationship.

Similar to linear regression, polynomial regression also uses a cost function, typically the mean squared error (MSE), to find the optimal values of the coefficients (bi's). The goal is to minimize the MSE by adjusting the coefficients to obtain the best-fitting polynomial curve.

Polynomial regression allows for more flexibility in modeling nonlinear relationships, making it a valuable tool when the data exhibits complex patterns. However, one must be cautious when using high-degree polynomials, as they can lead to overfitting, where the model fits the noise in the data rather than the true underlying relationship.

To mitigate the risk of overfitting in polynomial regression, techniques such as regularization and cross-validation can be applied. Regularization adds a penalty term to the cost function, discouraging the model from assigning high weights to higher-degree polynomial terms. Cross-validation can help in selecting the appropriate degree of the polynomial that balances the bias-variance tradeoff and achieves the best generalization performance.

When comparing linear regression and polynomial regression, linear regression is simpler and interpretable, suitable for linear relationships between the input features and the output variable. It performs well when the data exhibits a linear trend and is less prone to overfitting. On the other hand, polynomial regression can capture more complex relationships and has greater flexibility in modeling nonlinear data patterns. However, it requires careful tuning to avoid overfitting and may become computationally expensive with high-degree polynomials.

In conclusion, linear regression and polynomial regression are two essential regression techniques in machine learning. Linear regression assumes a linear relationship between the input features and the output variable, while polynomial regression allows for modeling nonlinear relationships using polynomial functions of varying degrees. Linear regression is straightforward and interpretable, making it suitable for simple regression tasks with linear trends. Polynomial regression, on the other hand, is more flexible and can capture complex data patterns but requires careful tuning to avoid overfitting. The choice between linear and polynomial regression depends on the data's characteristics and the complexity of the relationship between the input features and the output variable. Both regression techniques play crucial roles in predictive modeling and have widespread applications across various domains.

1. Logistic Regression for Binary and Multiclass Classification

Logistic regression is a fundamental and widely used supervised learning algorithm for classification tasks in machine learning. Despite its name, logistic regression is a classification algorithm rather than a regression one. It is particularly suited for binary classification problems, where the goal is to predict one of two possible classes or labels, such as "yes" or "no," "spam" or "not spam," or "positive" or "negative." However, logistic regression can also be extended to handle multiclass classification problems, where there are more than two classes or labels.

Binary Logistic Regression:

In binary logistic regression, the output variable is binary, taking on one of two possible values, usually represented as 0 and 1. The algorithm models the probability of the positive class (class 1) as a function of the input features.

The output of the logistic regression model is a probability score between 0 and 1, which represents the likelihood of the input belonging to the positive class.

The core idea behind logistic regression is to model the relationship between the input features and the log-odds (logit) of the positive class. The log-odds is the logarithm of the ratio between the probability of the positive class and the probability of the negative class. The relationship between the log-odds and the input features is assumed to be linear, just like in linear regression. However, to ensure that the output remains in the range of [0, 1], the logistic function (sigmoid function) is applied to the linear combination of the input features.

The logistic function is defined as $\sigma(z) = 1 / (1 + e^{(-z)})$, where z is the linear combination of the input features and the model's parameters. The output of the logistic function ($\sigma(z)$) represents the probability that the input belongs to the positive class, and $1 - \sigma(z)$

represents the probability of belonging to the negative class.

During training, the logistic regression model's parameters are estimated using an optimization algorithm that minimizes a cost function, typically the log-loss (cross-entropy) function. The log-loss measures the dissimilarity between the predicted probabilities and the true labels in the training data. The goal is to find the model's parameters that minimize the log-loss, maximizing the likelihood of the observed data.

Once the model is trained, it can be used to predict the class label of new, unseen data. The predicted class is determined based on a threshold (usually 0.5). If the predicted probability is greater than or equal to the threshold, the input is classified as the positive class (1); otherwise, it is classified as the negative class (0).

Multiclass Logistic Regression (Softmax Regression):

While binary logistic regression deals with two classes, multiclass logistic regression (also known as softmax regression) extends the algorithm to handle multiple classes. In a multiclass classification problem, the output variable can take on more than two possible classes or labels. The goal of softmax regression is to model the probabilities of all classes as a function of the input features and assign the input to the class with the highest probability.

In softmax regression, each class has its set of parameters (coefficients), and the model outputs a vector of probabilities corresponding to each class. The softmax function is applied to the linear combination of the input features and the class-specific parameters to transform the scores into probabilities that sum up to 1. The softmax function is defined as follows:

$P(class_i) = e^{z_i} / \Sigma(e^{z_j})$ for all j,

where $P(class_i)$ is the probability of the input belonging to class i, z_i is the linear combination of the input features and the parameters for class i, and $\Sigma(e^{(z_j)})$ is the sum of the exponentials of all class scores.

During training, softmax regression is optimized using the cross-entropy loss function, also known as the log-loss. The log-loss measures the dissimilarity between the predicted probabilities and the true one-hot encoded labels in the training data.

The optimization algorithm aims to find the model's parameters that minimize the log-loss and maximize the likelihood of the observed data. Once trained, the softmax regression model can be used to predict the class label of new, unseen data. The predicted class is determined based on the class with the highest probability score in the output vector.

One-vs-Rest (OvR) and One-vs-One (OvO) Strategies:

When dealing with multiclass classification, two common strategies are used to adapt binary logistic regression for multiclass problems: one-vs-rest (OvR) and one-vs-one (OvO).

In the one-vs-rest strategy, a separate binary logistic regression model is trained for each class, treating that class as the positive class and the rest of the classes as the negative class. During prediction, all binary models are applied to the input, and the class with the highest probability is selected as the predicted class. One-vs-rest is computationally efficient, especially for a large number of classes, as it requires training only C binary models for C classes.

In the one-vs-one strategy, a binary logistic regression model is trained for every pair of classes, classifying inputs into one class or the other. During prediction, each binary model votes on the input's class, and the class with the most votes is selected as the predicted class. One-vs-one requires training C * (C - 1) / 2 binary models for C classes, which can be computationally expensive, especially for a large number of classes. However, one-vs-one may perform better when some classes are more difficult to distinguish from others.

In conclusion, logistic regression is a widely used classification algorithm in machine learning, suitable for both binary and multiclass classification tasks. For binary classification, logistic regression models the probability of the positive class using the sigmoid function. For multiclass classification, softmax regression extends logistic regression to handle multiple classes, modeling the probabilities of all classes using the softmax function. Logistic regression is interpretable, computationally efficient, and can provide valuable insights into the relationship between the input features and the class labels. However, like any machine learning algorithm, the performance of logistic regression depends on the quality and quantity of the training data and appropriate hyperparameter tuning.

1. Decision Trees and Random Forests

Decision trees and random forests are powerful and versatile machine learning algorithms used for both classification and regression tasks. They are part of the ensemble learning family, which combines the predictions of multiple models to improve overall performance. Decision trees and random forests are widely used in various fields due to their interpretability, ability to handle both categorical and numerical data, and effectiveness in capturing complex relationships in the data.

Decision Trees:

A decision tree is a tree-like structure where each internal node represents a test on an input feature, each branch represents the outcome of the test, and each leaf node represents the final decision or prediction. The tree is constructed by recursively partitioning the data based on the input features to minimize the impurity or increase the information gain at each level.

The process of constructing a decision tree involves selecting the best feature and the corresponding threshold that splits the data into subsets with the highest information gain or purity. Information gain measures how much the knowledge of a particular feature reduces the uncertainty in predicting the class labels. Gini impurity and entropy are common metrics used to quantify the impurity or purity of the data.

During the tree construction, the algorithm searches for the feature and threshold that maximizes the information gain or minimizes the impurity at each node. This process is repeated until a stopping criterion is met, such as reaching a maximum depth or having a minimum number of data points in each leaf node.

Decision trees are easy to interpret and visualize, making them valuable for understanding the decision-making process in the model. However, decision trees can suffer from overfitting, especially if they are allowed to grow too deep, capturing noise and spurious patterns in the data.

Random Forests:

Random forests are an ensemble learning method that combines multiple decision trees to improve prediction accuracy and reduce overfitting. The basic idea behind random forests is to build multiple decision trees using random subsets of the data and features and then combine their predictions to make the final decision.

The random subsets of data are obtained through a process called bootstrapping, where a random sample with replacement is taken from the original training data. This process creates multiple datasets with variations, allowing the decision trees to capture different aspects of the data's underlying patterns.

Additionally, during the construction of each decision tree in the random forest, a random subset of features is considered at each node.

This feature subsampling ensures that each tree uses only a subset of the available features, reducing the correlation between the trees and promoting diversity.

After building all the decision trees, the predictions of each tree are aggregated to make the final prediction. For binary classification, the majority vote is used, where the predicted class is the one that receives the most votes from the individual decision trees. For regression tasks, the final prediction is the average of the predictions from all the trees.

The random forest algorithm's ability to reduce overfitting and improve prediction accuracy makes it a popular choice for many real-world applications. Moreover, random forests are robust to noisy and irrelevant features, making them suitable for high-dimensional datasets with many input features.

Random forests can also provide a measure of feature importance, which helps identify the most informative features for making predictions. The importance of a feature is computed by measuring how much the prediction accuracy decreases when the values of that feature are randomly permuted.

Despite their effectiveness, random forests can be computationally expensive and may require more memory compared to individual decision trees. Additionally, random forests' interpretability is lower than that of individual decision trees, as the combination of multiple trees makes it challenging to understand the entire model's decision-making process.

In conclusion, decision trees and random forests are powerful machine learning algorithms used for both classification and regression tasks. Decision trees provide interpretable models by recursively partitioning the data based on input features. However, they can be prone to overfitting. Random forests address this issue by aggregating predictions from multiple decision trees built on bootstrapped data and feature subsets, resulting in improved accuracy and reduced overfitting. Random forests are widely used in practice due to their ability to handle complex datasets, provide feature importance, and offer strong performance across a range of applications. However, their interpretability is reduced compared to individual decision trees. By understanding the strengths and limitations of decision trees and random forests, data scientists can leverage these algorithms effectively in various machine learning tasks.

Chapter 14: Unsupervised Learning: Clustering and Dimensionality Reduction

1. K-Means Clustering

K-Means clustering is a popular unsupervised machine learning algorithm used for partitioning data into K clusters based on similarity. Clustering is a technique used to group similar data points together while separating different groups from each other. K-Means is widely used in various domains, including data analysis, image segmentation, customer segmentation, and anomaly detection. The algorithm is relatively simple yet effective in identifying natural groupings within the data.

A. Introduction to Clustering:

Clustering is an unsupervised learning technique that aims to divide a dataset into distinct groups or clusters based on similarities among data points. Unlike supervised learning, clustering does not require labeled data; instead, it seeks to discover underlying patterns and structures in the data. The goal of clustering is to group similar data points together in the same cluster while ensuring that data points in different clusters are dissimilar. Clustering is particularly useful in scenarios where the data lacks clear target labels, making it challenging to use classification or regression algorithms.

B. The K-Means Algorithm:

The K-Means algorithm is a simple and efficient clustering technique that seeks to partition data into K clusters, where K is a user-defined hyperparameter. The algorithm starts by randomly selecting K points from the dataset as initial cluster centers, often referred to as centroids. These initial centroids act as representatives for the initial clusters.

The algorithm then proceeds through an iterative process of assigning each data point to the nearest centroid and recalculating the centroids based on the data points assigned to each cluster. This process is repeated until the centroids stabilize, and data points no longer switch clusters significantly.

C. Distance Metric and Assignment Step:

The distance metric used to determine the similarity between data points and centroids is usually the Euclidean distance, although other distance metrics, such as Manhattan distance or cosine similarity, can also be used. In the assignment step, each data point is assigned to the cluster whose centroid is the closest (i.e., has the minimum distance). This assignment step ensures that data points with similar features are grouped together, creating distinct clusters.

D. Update Step and Centroid Recalculation:

After assigning each data point to the nearest centroid, the algorithm proceeds to the update step, where it recalculates the centroids based on the data points in each cluster. The new centroids are computed as the mean of the data points' coordinates within the cluster. This centroid recalculation ensures that the cluster centers are representative of the data points within each cluster and helps improve the clustering quality.

E. Convergence and Termination:

The K-Means algorithm iterates between the assignment and update steps until convergence. Convergence occurs when the centroids stabilize, and there are no significant changes in the data points' cluster assignments. At this stage, the algorithm terminates, and the final clusters are formed.

F. Choosing the Value of K:

One of the challenges in using the K-Means algorithm is determining the appropriate value of K, the number of clusters. An optimal value of K is often problem-specific and may require domain knowledge or exploration of the data. There are several methods to find the optimal value of K, such as the Elbow method, Silhouette score, or Gap statistic. These methods help identify the K value that results in a well-defined and meaningful clustering solution.

G. Advantages and Limitations of K-Means Clustering:

K-Means clustering has several advantages, such as its simplicity, scalability to large datasets, and efficiency in handling high-dimensional data. It can be applied to various types of data, including numerical and categorical data, and it is relatively easy to implement. K-Means can handle large datasets with moderate computational resources and is often the first choice for many clustering applications.

However, K-Means has certain limitations that users should be aware of. Firstly, the algorithm is sensitive to the initial placement of the centroids, and different initializations can result in different clustering outcomes. To mitigate this issue, the algorithm is often run multiple times with different initializations, and the best clustering solution is selected based on a predefined criterion. Secondly, K-Means assumes that clusters are spherical and equally sized, which may not always hold in complex datasets with irregularly shaped or unevenly distributed clusters. In such cases, more advanced clustering algorithms, such as density-based clustering or hierarchical clustering, may be more appropriate.

In conclusion, K-Means clustering is a popular unsupervised learning algorithm used for partitioning data into K clusters based on similarity. The algorithm iteratively assigns data points to the nearest centroids and recalculates centroids until convergence, forming distinct clusters. K-Means is efficient and scalable, making it suitable for a wide range of clustering applications. However, users should be cautious about the sensitivity to initializations and the assumption of spherical clusters. By understanding the principles and considerations of K-Means clustering, data scientists can effectively apply this algorithm to uncover meaningful patterns and structures in their data.

1. Hierarchical Clustering

Hierarchical clustering is a popular unsupervised machine learning technique used for grouping data points into a hierarchical structure of nested clusters. Unlike other clustering algorithms like K-Means, hierarchical clustering does not require specifying the number of clusters beforehand. Instead, it organizes data points into a tree-like structure called a dendrogram, which provides a visual representation of the clustering process at different levels of granularity. Hierarchical clustering is widely used in various fields, including biology, social sciences, image segmentation, and data analysis.

A. Introduction to Hierarchical Clustering:

Clustering is an unsupervised learning technique that aims to group similar data points together and separate dissimilar data points. Hierarchical clustering is one of the fundamental clustering methods that create a hierarchical representation of the data based on similarity. It starts with each data point forming its cluster and then merges clusters iteratively to form a tree-like structure called a dendrogram. The dendrogram visualizes the clustering process and allows users to identify natural groupings in the data at different levels of granularity.

B. Agglomerative and Divisive Hierarchical Clustering:

There are two main approaches to hierarchical clustering: agglomerative and divisive. Agglomerative hierarchical clustering begins with each data point as a separate cluster and then merges the most similar clusters until all data points are in a single cluster. In contrast, divisive hierarchical clustering starts with all data points in a single cluster and then repeatedly divides the cluster into smaller clusters based on dissimilarity.

Agglomerative clustering is more commonly used due to its efficiency and ability to handle large datasets. It starts with a bottom-up approach, where individual data points are merged into clusters and then further merged until a single cluster is formed. The result is a dendrogram that represents the hierarchical structure of the data.

C. Distance Metric and Similarity Measures:

The first step in hierarchical clustering is to define a distance metric or similarity measure to quantify the similarity or dissimilarity between data points. The choice of distance metric depends on the nature of the data. For numerical data, the most common distance metric is the Euclidean distance, while for categorical data, other similarity measures like the Jaccard coefficient or Hamming distance may be used.

D. Merging Criteria:

During the agglomerative clustering process, clusters are merged based on a merging criterion that defines the distance between clusters. There are different methods to calculate the distance between clusters, such as single linkage, complete linkage, average linkage, and Ward's linkage.

- ***Single Linkage:*** The distance between two clusters is defined as the shortest distance between any two data points in the two clusters. It tends to form elongated clusters and is sensitive to noise and outliers.

- ***Complete Linkage:*** The distance between two clusters is defined as the maximum distance between any two data points in the two clusters. It tends to form compact and well-separated clusters.

- ***Average Linkage:*** The distance between two clusters is defined as the average distance between all pairs of data points in the two clusters. It strikes a balance between single and complete linkage.

- ***Ward's Linkage:*** Ward's method minimizes the variance within clusters during the merging process, aiming to create compact and evenly sized clusters.

E. Dendrogram Visualization:

The hierarchical clustering process results in a dendrogram, which is a tree-like diagram that represents the clustering structure. The dendrogram has a vertical axis that represents the distance or similarity between clusters, and a horizontal axis that represents individual data points or clusters. The height of the vertical lines in the dendrogram corresponds to the distance between clusters or data points. By cutting the dendrogram at a certain height, different numbers of clusters can be obtained, allowing users to explore clusters at different levels of granularity.

F. Determining the Number of Clusters:

One of the challenges in hierarchical clustering is determining the appropriate number of clusters. The dendrogram provides a visual tool to help users decide on the optimal number of clusters based on the height at which the dendrogram is cut. The height at which the dendrogram is cut corresponds to the distance or dissimilarity between clusters. The decision on the number of clusters may also depend on the specific application and domain knowledge.

G. Advantages and Limitations of Hierarchical Clustering:

Hierarchical clustering has several advantages, such as its ability to capture complex relationships in the data, its interpretability through dendrogram visualization, and its flexibility in handling different types of distance metrics. Additionally, hierarchical clustering does not require specifying the number of clusters beforehand, making it suitable for exploratory data analysis.

However, hierarchical clustering can be computationally expensive, especially for large datasets, as the complexity increases with the number of data points. The construction of the dendrogram can be memory-intensive, making it less scalable for big data applications. Additionally, hierarchical clustering may not be suitable for datasets with irregularly shaped clusters or noise, as it tends to form elongated clusters in some cases.

In conclusion, hierarchical clustering is a powerful unsupervised learning technique used for grouping data points into a hierarchical structure of nested clusters. It provides a dendrogram visualization that allows users to explore the clustering structure at different levels of granularity. The choice of distance metric and merging criteria impacts the resulting clustering. Hierarchical clustering is widely used for understanding data patterns, identifying natural groupings, and facilitating data exploration and analysis. Despite its computational limitations for large datasets, hierarchical clustering remains a valuable tool in a data scientist's toolkit for various clustering tasks.

1. Principal Component Analysis (PCA) for Dimensionality Reduction

Principal Component Analysis (PCA) is a popular dimensionality reduction technique used in machine learning and data analysis to transform high-dimensional data into a lower-dimensional space. It accomplishes this by identifying the principal components, which are orthogonal directions capturing the most significant variance in the data. PCA is widely used for data visualization, noise reduction, and improving the performance of machine learning algorithms by reducing the number of features.

A. Introduction to Dimensionality Reduction:

Dimensionality reduction is a crucial preprocessing step in machine learning and data analysis when dealing with high-dimensional datasets. High-dimensional data can suffer from the curse of dimensionality, which leads to increased computational complexity, overfitting, and difficulty in interpreting the data. Dimensionality reduction aims to reduce the number of features while preserving the essential information and patterns in the data. This allows for easier visualization, faster computations, and improved generalization performance of machine learning models.

B. Principal Component Analysis (PCA) Overview:

PCA is a linear dimensionality reduction technique that transforms high-dimensional data into a new coordinate system that is aligned with the directions of maximum variance in the data. These new coordinates are referred to as principal components. The first principal component accounts for the most significant variance in the data, the second principal component accounts for the second most significant variance, and so on.

The principal components are orthogonal to each other, meaning they are uncorrelated. This orthogonality property ensures that each principal component captures unique information from the data. PCA finds these principal components by performing an eigendecomposition or singular value decomposition (SVD) on the covariance matrix or the data matrix.

C. Steps of PCA:

The PCA algorithm involves several steps:

- ***Mean Centering:*** In the first step, the mean of each feature in the dataset is subtracted from the corresponding data points. This process is called mean centering and is necessary to center the data around the origin.

- ***Covariance Matrix or Data Matrix:*** Depending on the choice of PCA implementation, a covariance matrix or data matrix is computed. The covariance matrix represents the pairwise covariances between the features in the data, while the data matrix is formed by stacking the mean-centered data points as rows.

- ***Eigendecomposition or SVD:*** The next step is to perform an eigendecomposition or SVD on the covariance matrix or the data matrix. This process calculates the eigenvalues and eigenvectors of the matrix. The eigenvalues represent the variance explained by each principal component, while the eigenvectors are the directions of the principal components.

- ***Selecting Principal Components:*** The principal components are sorted in descending order of their corresponding eigenvalues, indicating the amount of variance they explain. The first few principal components with the highest eigenvalues are selected to represent the most significant variance in the data.

D. Dimensionality Reduction:

The selected principal components are used to form a projection matrix, where each row corresponds to a principal component. By multiplying the projection matrix with the mean-centered data, a lower-dimensional representation of the data is obtained. The number of principal components chosen determines the dimensionality of the reduced space.

The dimensionality reduction process enables data to be represented in a lower-dimensional space, where each dimension is a principal component representing the most important information from the original high-dimensional data.

E. Explained Variance and Retained Information:

A crucial aspect of PCA is the explained variance, which quantifies the proportion of total variance captured by each principal component. The cumulative sum of explained variances provides insights into how much information is retained as the number of principal components increases. Data scientists can use this information to decide the appropriate number of principal components that sufficiently capture the essential information while reducing the dimensionality.

F. PCA for Data Visualization and Noise Reduction:

One of the significant benefits of PCA is its utility for data visualization. By reducing data to two or three principal components, high-dimensional data can be visualized in a scatter plot, enabling the identification of patterns, clusters, and relationships between data points.

Moreover, PCA can act as a noise reduction technique. By representing data in a lower-dimensional space, the influence of noisy or less informative features is reduced, improving the overall robustness of the data representation.

G. PCA for Feature Selection and Compression:

PCA can also be leveraged for feature selection. It allows for the identification of the most relevant features by examining the principal components' corresponding loadings (coefficients). Features with higher loadings have a more substantial impact on the principal components and, therefore, contribute more to the data's variance. Selecting features based on loadings can lead to more interpretable models and improve generalization.

Additionally, PCA can be used for data compression. By keeping only a subset of the principal components, the data is compressed into a lower-dimensional representation, resulting in reduced memory requirements and faster computation.

H. Limitations of PCA:

While PCA is a powerful technique for dimensionality reduction, it has some limitations. Notably, PCA assumes linearity in the data. If the underlying data relationships are nonlinear, PCA may not capture the essential structure adequately. In such cases, nonlinear dimensionality reduction techniques, such as t-distributed Stochastic Neighbor Embedding (t-SNE) or Isomap, may be more appropriate.

Another limitation is that PCA is sensitive to the scale of the data. It is essential to standardize or normalize the features before applying PCA to ensure that each feature contributes equally to the principal components.

In conclusion, Principal Component Analysis (PCA) is a widely used dimensionality reduction technique in machine learning and data analysis. By finding the principal components that capture the most significant variance in the data, PCA transforms high-dimensional data into a lower-dimensional space. It offers benefits such as data visualization, noise reduction, and feature selection, making it a valuable tool for data preprocessing and analysis. However, users should be aware of its assumptions, limitations, and the need for scaling the data appropriately. By understanding PCA's principles and considerations, data scientists can effectively leverage this technique to enhance data analysis and improve machine learning model performance.

Chapter 15: Evaluation Metrics for Machine Learning Models

1. Accuracy, Precision, Recall, and F1 Score

In the realm of machine learning, the performance of a model is often assessed through various metrics, including Accuracy, Precision, Recall, and F1 Score. These metrics play a crucial role in evaluating the effectiveness and reliability of a model's predictions. Each metric represents a different aspect of the model's performance and is used to assess its suitability for specific tasks and applications.

Accuracy:

Accuracy is one of the most commonly used metrics in machine learning. It measures the proportion of correct predictions made by the model over the total number of predictions. Mathematically, it can be expressed as:

Accuracy= Total Number of Predictions / Number of Correct Predictions

While accuracy provides an overall performance measure, it might not be sufficient when dealing with imbalanced datasets, where one class significantly outnumbers the others. In such cases, a high accuracy value can be misleading since the model might be biased towards the majority class, making it perform poorly on the minority class.

Precision:

Precision is a metric that focuses on the correctness of positive predictions made by the model. It quantifies the proportion of true positive predictions (correctly identified positive instances) over the total number of positive predictions (both true positives and false positives). Precision is particularly valuable when the cost of false positives is high. Mathematically, it can be expressed as:

Precision= True Positives / True Positives + False Positives

A high precision value indicates that the model is accurate in identifying positive instances, minimizing the occurrence of false positives.

Recall (Sensitivity or True Positive Rate):

Recall measures the model's ability to correctly identify positive instances from the total number of actual positive instances. It quantifies the proportion of true positive predictions over the total number of positive instances (true positives and false negatives). Recall is crucial when the cost of false negatives is high, as it ensures that positive cases are not missed. Mathematically, it can be expressed as:

Recall= True Positives / True Positives + False negatives

A high recall value indicates that the model is capable of identifying most of the positive instances present in the dataset.

F1 Score:

The F1 Score is a combination of precision and recall and is often used when there is a need for a balance between these two metrics. It is the harmonic mean of precision and recall, providing a single value that considers both false positives and false negatives. The F1 Score is useful when there is an uneven class distribution in the dataset. Mathematically, it can be expressed as:

F1 Score= 2×Precision×Recall / Precision + Recall

The F1 Score penalizes models that have imbalanced precision and recall, thus encouraging a more balanced performance.

In summary, Accuracy, Precision, Recall, and F1 Score are essential metrics in machine learning that provide valuable insights into the model's performance. Each metric serves a specific purpose, and the choice of which to emphasize depends on the nature of the problem and the associated costs of false positives and false negatives. While Accuracy provides an overall view of the model's performance, Precision, Recall, and F1 Score offer a more detailed analysis of its abilities to handle positive and negative instances. Machine learning practitioners often consider these metrics together to get a comprehensive understanding of their models and make informed decisions for further improvements.

1. Confusion Matrix and ROC Curve

Confusion Matrix:

The confusion matrix is a fundamental tool used to assess the performance of a machine learning model, particularly in the context of classification tasks. It provides a comprehensive and detailed summary of the model's predictions compared to the actual ground truth. The matrix is constructed by organizing the predicted outcomes into four categories: true positives (TP), false positives (FP), true negatives (TN), and false negatives (FN).

- ***True Positives (TP):*** These are the cases where the model correctly predicts the positive class (e.g., correctly identifying a disease in a medical diagnosis).

- ***False Positives (FP):*** These are the cases where the model incorrectly predicts the positive class when the actual class is negative (e.g., predicting a disease when it is not present).

- ***True Negatives (TN):*** These are the cases where the model correctly predicts the negative class (e.g., correctly identifying a non-disease case in a medical diagnosis).

- ***False Negatives (FN):*** These are the cases where the model incorrectly predicts the negative class when the actual class is positive (e.g., missing a disease that is actually present).

The confusion matrix is usually presented in a tabular format, making it easy to interpret and analyze the model's performance. With the confusion matrix, various performance metrics can be derived, including accuracy, precision, recall (sensitivity), specificity, and the F1 score, which were discussed in the previous explanation.

ROC Curve (Receiver Operating Characteristic Curve):

The ROC curve is a graphical representation used to assess and compare the performance of binary classification models. It illustrates the trade-off between the true positive rate (recall or sensitivity) and the false positive rate (1-specificity) at various classification thresholds. The ROC curve is particularly useful when evaluating models that have varying classification thresholds, as it provides a more nuanced understanding of their performance across different decision points.

To construct an ROC curve, the model's predictions are sorted based on their probability scores or confidence levels. The threshold is then adjusted gradually, and at each threshold, the true positive rate (TPR) and false positive rate (FPR) are calculated. The TPR is the proportion of true positive predictions, while the FPR is the proportion of false positive predictions. These values are plotted on the y-axis and x-axis, respectively, to form the ROC curve.

An ideal ROC curve is one that hugs the top-left corner, indicating a high true positive rate and a low false positive rate, regardless of the classification threshold. Such a curve represents a model with excellent discriminatory power. On the other hand, a random classifier's ROC curve is a diagonal line from the bottom-left to the top-right corner, as it has equal chances of true positive and false positive predictions across all thresholds.

Area Under the ROC Curve (AUC):

The Area Under the ROC Curve (AUC) is a scalar metric that quantifies the overall performance of a binary classification model. It represents the area under the ROC curve and provides a single value to compare the discriminative power of different models. A perfect classifier has an AUC value of 1, while a random classifier has an AUC of 0.5.

A higher AUC indicates that the model can effectively distinguish between positive and negative instances, making it more suitable for the given classification task. In practice, an AUC value above 0.8 is often considered indicative of a good model, while an

AUC below 0.7 might require further improvement.

<u>Interpreting the ROC Curve and AUC:</u>

The ROC curve allows machine learning practitioners to visualize the performance of their models across different classification thresholds. By comparing multiple ROC curves, one can determine which model performs better, depending on the task's requirements and the associated costs of false positives and false negatives. A model that consistently outperforms others at various thresholds and has a higher AUC is generally preferred for most applications.

In summary, the confusion matrix and ROC curve are vital tools in evaluating the performance of machine learning models, especially in binary classification tasks. The confusion matrix provides a detailed breakdown of the model's predictions, allowing for the calculation of various performance metrics. On the other hand, the ROC curve provides a visual representation of the model's performance across different classification thresholds, with the AUC providing a single-value summary of the model's overall performance. These tools aid in understanding the strengths and weaknesses of the model, guiding further improvements to achieve better results in real-world applications.

1. Regression Metrics: MSE, MAE, and R-squared

In machine learning, regression is a type of supervised learning where the goal is to predict continuous numeric values. To assess the performance of regression models, various evaluation metrics are used, including Mean Squared Error (MSE), Mean Absolute Error (MAE), and R-squared (R^2). These metrics help measure the accuracy and goodness of fit of the model's predictions to the actual target values.

Mean Squared Error (MSE):

Mean Squared Error (MSE) is one of the most commonly used metrics to evaluate regression models. It measures the average squared difference between the predicted values and the actual target values. The MSE provides a quantitative measure of the model's accuracy, with lower values indicating better performance.

Mathematically, MSE is calculated as follows:

$$\text{MSE} = \frac{1}{n}\sum_{i=1}^{n}(y_i - \hat{y}_i)^2$$

Where:

- n is the number of data points in the dataset.
- y_i represents the actual target value of the i-th data point.
- $\hat{y}_i$ represents the predicted value of the i-th data point.

Since the differences are squared before taking the mean, MSE tends to penalize larger prediction errors more severely, making it sensitive to outliers in the data.

Mean Absolute Error (MAE):

Mean Absolute Error (MAE) is another regression metric used to measure the accuracy of the model's predictions. Unlike MSE, MAE computes the average absolute difference between the predicted values and the actual target values. MAE is less sensitive to outliers compared to MSE because it does not square the differences.

Mathematically, MAE is calculated as follows:

$$\text{MAE} = \frac{1}{n}\sum_{i=1}^{n} |y_i - \hat{y}_i|$$

Where all variables have the same meaning as in the MSE formula.

MAE provides a more intuitive representation of the average prediction error, and its value is directly interpretable in the unit of the target variable. It is often used in situations where outliers are of particular interest and should not be overly penalized.

R-squared (R^2):

R-squared (R^2), also known as the coefficient of determination, is a metric used to evaluate the goodness of fit of a regression model. It represents the proportion of the variance in the dependent variable (target) that is explained by the independent variables (features) in the model. R-squared values range from 0 to 1, with 1 indicating a perfect fit and 0 indicating that the model does not explain any variance in the target variable.

Mathematically, R-squared is calculated as follows:

$$R^2 = 1 - \frac{\sum_{i=1}^{n}(y_i - \hat{y}_i)^2}{\sum_{i=1}^{n}(y_i - \bar{y})^2}$$

Where:

- n is the number of data points in the dataset.
- y_i represents the actual target value of the i-th data point.
- $\hat{y}_i$ represents the predicted value of the i-th data point.
- $\bar{y}$ represents the mean of the actual target values.

R-squared provides an assessment of how well the model's predictions match the variability of the target variable. A higher R-squared value indicates that the model explains a larger proportion of the variance in the target variable, suggesting a better fit. However, R-squared can be misleading when used inappropriately, especially when the number of features in the model is increased.

Interpreting Regression Metrics:

When evaluating regression models, it is essential to consider multiple metrics to gain a comprehensive understanding of their performance. MSE and MAE provide information about the average prediction error, with MSE being more sensitive to outliers due to the squared differences. MAE is generally preferred when outliers are a concern or when the absolute magnitude of the errors is crucial.

R-squared, on the other hand, assesses the overall goodness of fit of the model. A high R-squared value indicates that the model's predictions closely match the variability in the target variable. However, it is important to be cautious when using R-squared alone, as it may not capture all aspects of the model's performance, especially if the model is complex or overfitting the data.

In conclusion, regression metrics such as MSE, MAE, and R-squared are essential tools for evaluating the accuracy and performance of regression models in machine learning. Each metric provides unique insights into the model's predictive capabilities, and considering them together allows for a more robust assessment of the model's strengths and weaknesses. Careful consideration of these metrics helps in selecting the most suitable regression model for a given task and making informed decisions for model improvement.

Unit V: Advanced Machine Learning Techniques

Machine Learning (ML) has revolutionized various industries by enabling systems to learn patterns and make predictions from data without being explicitly programmed. While traditional ML methods like linear regression and decision trees have proven effective in many scenarios, the field has evolved to encompass more sophisticated techniques that tackle complex problems and leverage large datasets. Advanced Machine Learning Techniques refer to a set of powerful algorithms and methodologies that go beyond basic ML approaches and address intricate challenges in fields like computer vision, natural language processing, recommendation systems, and more.

- ***Deep Learning:***

Deep Learning is a subset of ML that involves artificial neural networks, inspired by the human brain's structure. These networks consist of multiple layers of interconnected nodes, also known as neurons. Each layer processes data and passes it to the next, ultimately leading to feature extraction and prediction. The use of deep neural networks has enabled breakthroughs in image and speech recognition, language translation, and many other tasks.

- ***Convolutional Neural Networks (CNNs):***

CNNs are a class of deep neural networks specifically designed for computer vision tasks. They employ convolutional layers to automatically learn hierarchical representations from images. These networks have shown exceptional performance in image classification, object detection, and semantic segmentation tasks.

- ***Recurrent Neural Networks (RNNs):***

RNNs are designed to process sequential data, such as time series or natural language. They utilize feedback loops that allow information persistence across time steps, making them suitable for tasks like language modeling, machine translation, and sentiment analysis.

- ***Generative Adversarial Networks (GANs):***

GANs are a unique class of deep learning models that consist of two neural networks: a generator and a discriminator. The generator generates synthetic data, while the discriminator tries to distinguish between real and fake data. The interplay between these networks results in the generation of high-quality synthetic data, leading to applications in image synthesis, data augmentation, and generating realistic content.

- ***Transfer Learning:***

Transfer learning is a technique where a pre-trained ML model is used as the starting point for a new task. By leveraging knowledge learned from a large dataset on a related problem, transfer learning can significantly reduce the amount of data and time required to train a model for a new task. It is especially beneficial in scenarios where labeled data is scarce.

- ***Reinforcement Learning (RL):***

Reinforcement Learning is a type of ML where an agent learns to take actions in an environment to maximize a reward signal. The agent explores the environment through trial and error, learning optimal strategies and policies. RL has found success in areas such as autonomous vehicles, game playing (e.g., AlphaGo), and robotics.

- ***Bayesian Methods:***

Bayesian methods provide a probabilistic framework for ML, allowing for uncertainty estimation and improved decision-making. Bayesian models can incorporate prior knowledge and update beliefs based on observed data, making them particularly useful when data is limited or noisy.

- ***Autoencoders and Variational Autoencoders (VAEs):***

Autoencoders are a type of neural network that learns to reconstruct the input data. They are used for tasks like dimensionality reduction, anomaly detection, and denoising data. VAEs are a variation of autoencoders that learn to generate new data points from a given distribution, enabling the creation of novel and diverse samples.

- ***Ensemble Methods:***

Ensemble methods combine predictions from multiple ML models to achieve better performance than any single model. Techniques like bagging, boosting, and stacking can enhance the overall predictive accuracy and robustness of ML systems.

- ***Attention Mechanisms:***

Attention mechanisms are widely used in sequence-to-sequence models and have greatly improved the performance of various NLP tasks.

They allow the model to focus on relevant parts of the input while processing sequential data, resulting in more accurate and contextually relevant outputs.

In conclusion, Advanced Machine Learning Techniques represent a diverse set of powerful tools that have pushed the boundaries of what ML can achieve. These methodologies have enabled groundbreaking advancements in various domains, making it possible to address complex challenges and deliver more accurate and sophisticated solutions. As the field of ML continues to evolve, these techniques will likely continue to play a pivotal role in shaping the future of technology and AI-driven applications.

Chapter 16: Ensembles and Boosting Algorithms

1. Bagging and Boosting Concepts

Machine learning algorithms are powerful tools used to make predictions, classify data, and extract patterns from vast amounts of information. Bagging and Boosting are two popular ensemble learning techniques that aim to improve the performance of individual models by combining their outputs. These techniques are widely used in various fields, including computer vision, natural language processing, and financial forecasting. In this comprehensive guide, we will delve into the concepts of Bagging and Boosting, exploring their fundamental principles, applications, and comparative insights.

A. Bagging: Bootstrap Aggregating

Bagging, short for Bootstrap Aggregating, is an ensemble learning method that involves building multiple independent models and combining their predictions to arrive at a final output. The fundamental idea behind bagging is to introduce diversity among the individual models, reducing the variance of the overall prediction. The process starts by creating several subsets (bags) of the training data, each containing a random sample with replacement. This means that some instances may appear multiple times in a single subset, while others may not appear at all. Each of these subsets is then used to train a separate base model, typically using the same learning algorithm.

By training on different subsets, each base model develops unique perspectives and learns specific patterns in the data. As a result, they exhibit diverse strengths and weaknesses. During the prediction phase, bagging combines the outputs of these base models to reach a final consensus. In the case of regression tasks, the outputs are usually averaged, while for classification tasks, a majority voting scheme is employed.

B. Random Forest: A Popular Bagging Technique

One of the most well-known applications of bagging is the Random Forest algorithm. A Random Forest is an ensemble of decision trees, where each tree is trained on a different subset of the data using a random subset of features. The final prediction of the Random Forest is determined by aggregating the predictions of all the constituent decision trees. Random Forests are robust against overfitting and can handle high-dimensional data, making them popular for various tasks such as classification, regression, and feature importance ranking.

C. Advantages and Disadvantages of Bagging

Bagging offers several advantages that contribute to its popularity:

a. **Reduction of Variance:** By training multiple models on diverse subsets of data, bagging effectively reduces the variance of the predictions. This results in improved generalization and robustness.

b. Parallelization: The training of base models in bagging can be easily parallelized since each model is trained independently on a different subset. This makes bagging computationally efficient and scalable.

c. Robustness to Outliers: Bagging is less sensitive to outliers compared to single models, as the impact of individual predictions is diluted when combined.

However, bagging also has some limitations:

a. Limited Bias Reduction: While bagging helps to reduce variance, it may not significantly reduce bias in the individual models. If the base models are biased, the ensemble may still suffer from the same biases.

b. Interpretability: The final predictions of a bagged model are typically more challenging to interpret than those of individual models, as they involve the combination of multiple outputs.

D. Boosting: Iterative Model Improvement

Boosting is another ensemble learning technique that aims to improve the performance of weak learners by sequentially refining their predictions. Unlike bagging, boosting focuses on reducing both bias and variance by giving more weight to misclassified instances during training. Boosting algorithms create a sequence of base models, where each subsequent model tries to correct the errors made by the previous ones. This iterative process continues until a stopping criterion is met or until the model reaches a predefined number of iterations.

Boosting assigns higher weights to misclassified instances, effectively emphasizing the harder-to-predict samples. Consequently, the base models are incentivized to focus on the problematic areas of the data distribution, leading to a more accurate and robust final ensemble.

E. AdaBoost: Adaptive Boosting

AdaBoost (Adaptive Boosting) is a popular boosting algorithm that introduced the concept of weighting misclassified instances to improve the model's performance. In AdaBoost, the first base model is trained on the original data, and the misclassified instances are given higher weights for the subsequent model. This process continues, and each new model focuses on the previously misclassified instances, gradually improving the ensemble's predictive capabilities.

During the prediction phase, the output of each base model is combined using weighted voting, where models with lower error rates are assigned higher weights. AdaBoost is particularly useful for tasks like face detection, object recognition, and natural language processing.

F. Advantages and Disadvantages of Boosting

Boosting offers several advantages that make it a powerful technique:

a. *Better Accuracy:* Boosting significantly improves the accuracy of weak learners, leading to high-performing models that can outperform individual strong learners.

b. Robustness to Noise: The iterative nature of boosting allows the model to learn from its mistakes and be more robust to noisy data.

c. ***Efficiency in High-Dimensional Data:*** Boosting algorithms can effectively handle high-dimensional data and automatically select relevant features, reducing the risk of overfitting.

However, boosting also comes with some challenges:

a. Overfitting Risk: If the number of iterations is too high, boosting can overfit the training data and perform poorly on unseen data.

b. Computationally Expensive: Boosting often requires more computation and time compared to bagging, as the models are trained sequentially.

G. Bagging vs. Boosting: A Comparative Analysis

While both bagging and boosting aim to improve model performance through ensembling, they have distinct characteristics that influence their application:

a. ***Diversity in Training:*** Bagging generates diversity by training models on different subsets of data, while boosting focuses on emphasizing the misclassified instances to improve learning.

b. ***Variance vs. Bias Reduction:*** Bagging primarily reduces variance, making it beneficial when individual models tend to overfit. Boosting, on the other hand, targets both bias and variance, making it suitable for scenarios with underfitting models.

c. ***Model Parallelism:*** Bagging allows for easy parallelization of training, while boosting requires sequential model building, making it less parallel-friendly.

d. ***Performance:*** Boosting generally outperforms bagging when the base models are weak learners, but the choice between the two depends on the specific dataset and the learning task.

Bagging and boosting are two powerful ensemble learning techniques that have revolutionized the field of machine learning. Bagging leverages the idea of creating diverse models to reduce variance, while boosting iteratively improves weak learners to reduce both bias and variance. Understanding the principles, advantages, and limitations of bagging and boosting empowers data scientists and machine learning practitioners to choose the most appropriate technique for their specific applications. By harnessing the potential of these advanced machine learning techniques, we can build more accurate and robust predictive models to tackle real-world challenges.

1. Random Forests and Gradient Boosting

Machine learning has seen tremendous advancements over the years, with various algorithms designed to tackle complex problems and deliver accurate predictions. Random Forests and Gradient Boosting are two sophisticated techniques widely used in the field of machine learning for ensemble learning and improving model performance. Both methods are based on the idea of combining multiple weak learners to create powerful predictive models. In this comprehensive guide, we will delve into the concepts of Random Forests and Gradient Boosting, exploring their fundamental principles, differences, advantages, and applications.

A. Random Forests: A Powerful Ensemble Method

Random Forests are an ensemble learning technique based on the principle of bagging (Bootstrap Aggregating). This method involves the construction of multiple decision trees, where each tree is trained on a random subset of the training data and a random subset of features. The combination of these diverse decision trees leads to a robust and high-performing model.

- ***A.1. How Random Forests Work:***

a. Bootstrap Sampling: Random Forests employ bootstrap sampling, which means that each tree is trained on a random subset of the training data with replacement. This creates diverse subsets, ensuring that each tree learns from slightly different samples.

b. Random Feature Selection: During the construction of each decision tree, only a random subset of features is considered for splitting at each node. This further increases the diversity among the trees and prevents any single feature from dominating the decision-making process.

c. Voting or Averaging: For regression tasks, the outputs of individual trees are averaged, while for classification tasks, a majority voting scheme is employed to determine the final prediction of the Random Forest.

- ***Advantages of Random Forests:***

a. High Accuracy: Random Forests are known for their high accuracy and robustness against overfitting, making them suitable for a wide range of tasks.

b. Feature Importance: Random Forests provide a measure of feature importance, allowing us to identify the most influential features in the prediction process.

c. Scalability: Random Forests can handle large datasets and high-dimensional feature spaces effectively, making them suitable for real-world applications with complex data.

B. Gradient Boosting: Iterative Model Refinement

Gradient Boosting is another ensemble learning technique that aims to improve model performance by sequentially combining weak learners. Unlike Random Forests, which train multiple trees independently, Gradient Boosting builds decision trees in a sequential manner, with each tree focusing on correcting the errors made by the previous ones.

- ***<u>How Gradient Boosting Works:</u>***

a. ***Initial Model:*** Gradient Boosting starts by training an initial weak learner (usually a decision tree) on the training data.

b. ***Error Calculation:*** The errors or residuals from the first model are calculated for each data point. These residuals represent the difference between the true target values and the predictions made by the first model.

c. Sequential Tree Building: A new decision tree is then constructed to predict these residuals. This tree is fitted to the negative gradient of the loss function with respect to the previous model's output.

d. Model Combination: The predictions of the new tree are added to the predictions of the previous model, reducing the overall error.

e. Iterative Process: This process of calculating residuals, building a new tree, and combining models is repeated iteratively until a stopping criterion is met or a predefined number of trees are built.

- ***Advantages of Gradient Boosting:***

a. High Accuracy: Gradient Boosting often yields highly accurate predictions and can outperform Random Forests and other algorithms.

b. Handling Complex Patterns: Gradient Boosting is capable of capturing complex patterns in the data, making it suitable for challenging tasks.

c. ***Feature Importance:*** Similar to Random Forests, Gradient Boosting provides feature importance scores, helping us understand the model's decision-making process.

C. Random Forests vs. Gradient Boosting

While both Random Forests and Gradient Boosting are ensemble techniques that aim to improve model performance, they have several key differences:

a. *Independence vs. Sequential Learning:* Random Forests train individual decision trees independently, whereas Gradient Boosting builds trees in a sequential manner, with each tree trying to correct the errors of the previous ones.

b. *Diversity in Learning:* Random Forests achieve diversity through random sampling of data and features, while Gradient Boosting focuses on correcting errors by emphasizing misclassified instances.

c. *Parallelism:* Random Forests can be easily parallelized as the trees are independent, making them more efficient for distributed computing. Gradient Boosting, on the other hand, is inherently sequential, making it less parallel-friendly.

d. Bias-Variance Tradeoff: Random Forests primarily focus on reducing variance, making them suitable for tasks where overfitting is a concern. Gradient Boosting targets both bias and variance, making it well-suited for underfitting problems.

D. Applications of Random Forests and Gradient Boosting

Both Random Forests and Gradient Boosting find applications in various domains:

a. Random Forests: Due to their high accuracy and ability to handle complex data, Random Forests are widely used in fields like computer vision, bioinformatics, and finance for tasks such as image classification, protein structure prediction, and credit risk analysis.

b. Gradient Boosting: Gradient Boosting's superior performance and ability to capture intricate patterns make it well-suited for tasks like web search ranking, recommendation systems, and anomaly detection.

Random Forests and Gradient Boosting are two advanced machine learning techniques that leverage the power of ensemble learning to create high-performing predictive models. Random Forests excel at reducing variance and handling high-dimensional data, while Gradient Boosting focuses on iteratively refining weak learners to achieve high accuracy. By understanding the principles and characteristics of these techniques, data scientists can make informed choices when addressing complex real-world problems and unlock the full potential of ensemble learning in machine learning applications.

1. XGBoost and LightGBM

XGBoost and LightGBM are state-of-the-art machine learning algorithms that have gained immense popularity in the data science community due to their exceptional performance and efficiency. Both techniques are based on Gradient Boosting, which is an ensemble learning method that iteratively combines weak learners to create a powerful predictive model. In this comprehensive guide, we will delve into the concepts of XGBoost and LightGBM, exploring their fundamental principles, differences, advantages, and applications.

A. XGBoost: Extreme Gradient Boosting

XGBoost, short for Extreme Gradient Boosting, is an optimized implementation of the Gradient Boosting algorithm. Developed by Tianqi Chen in 2014, XGBoost is designed to be both highly accurate and computationally efficient. It introduces several innovations and enhancements over traditional Gradient Boosting, making it a top choice for various machine learning tasks.

- ***Key Features of XGBoost:***

a. Regularization: XGBoost includes L1 and L2 regularization terms in its objective function, preventing overfitting and improving generalization.

b. Handling Missing Values: XGBoost can automatically handle missing values in the dataset, sparing the need for data imputation.

c. ***Weighted Quantile Sketch:*** To improve the computational speed, XGBoost uses a weighted quantile sketch algorithm for histogram-based tree construction.

d. Cross-validation: XGBoost supports built-in cross-validation, enabling easy model evaluation and hyperparameter tuning.

- ***Advantages of XGBoost:***

a. ***High Performance:*** XGBoost's efficient implementation and optimization techniques make it one of the fastest and most powerful machine learning algorithms.

b. ***Regularization:*** The inclusion of regularization terms in the objective function helps prevent overfitting, enhancing the model's robustness.

c. ***Flexibility:*** XGBoost can handle various types of data, including numerical and categorical features, making it suitable for a wide range of tasks.

B. LightGBM: Light Gradient Boosting Machine

LightGBM is another Gradient Boosting-based algorithm that was introduced by Microsoft in 2017. It is designed to address the limitations of traditional Gradient Boosting algorithms and achieve faster training speed and lower memory usage while maintaining high accuracy.

- ***Key Features of LightGBM:***

a. ***Leaf-Wise Tree Growth:*** LightGBM adopts a leaf-wise tree growth strategy, as opposed to level-wise growth in traditional methods. This approach prioritizes nodes that can reduce the loss the most, leading to a more efficient and accurate model.

b. Gradient-Based One-Side Sampling: LightGBM uses gradient-based one-side sampling to choose the data instances with the largest gradients for constructing new trees. This accelerates the training process and enhances model performance.

c. Histogram-Based Approach: LightGBM employs a histogram-based approach for feature discretization, resulting in faster computation and reduced memory usage.

d. Categorical Feature Support: LightGBM efficiently handles categorical features without the need for one-hot encoding, saving memory and improving training speed.

- ***Advantages of LightGBM:***

a. Speed and Efficiency: LightGBM's leaf-wise tree growth and histogram-based approach lead to faster training times and reduced memory consumption.

b. Scalability: LightGBM can handle large datasets efficiently, making it suitable for big data applications.

c. High Accuracy: Despite its computational optimizations, LightGBM maintains high accuracy, often outperforming other Gradient Boosting algorithms.

C. XGBoost vs. LightGBM

Both XGBoost and LightGBM are powerful algorithms based on Gradient Boosting, but they have some notable differences:

a. Tree Growth Strategy: XGBoost uses a depth-wise tree growth strategy, while LightGBM employs a leaf-wise approach. This impacts the trade-off between speed and accuracy.

b. Memory Usage: LightGBM typically consumes less memory compared to XGBoost due to its histogram-based approach and efficient handling of categorical features.

c. Speed: LightGBM is generally faster during training due to its leaf-wise tree growth and gradient-based one-side sampling techniques.

d. Performance: While LightGBM is often faster, XGBoost might achieve slightly better accuracy on certain datasets, especially when the dataset is small or the feature space is not highly sparse.

D. Applications of XGBoost and LightGBM

Both XGBoost and LightGBM find applications in various domains:

a. XGBoost: XGBoost is widely used in diverse fields, including image classification, natural language processing, and financial modeling. Its speed and accuracy make it suitable for real-time applications and competitions on platforms like Kaggle.

b. LightGBM: LightGBM's efficiency and scalability make it particularly useful in scenarios involving large datasets and high-dimensional feature spaces. It is commonly used in online advertising, web search ranking, and recommendation systems.

XGBoost and LightGBM are two advanced machine learning algorithms that have transformed the landscape of ensemble learning and gradient boosting techniques. While XGBoost excels in accuracy and offers regularization, LightGBM stands out with its speed, memory efficiency, and scalable nature. The choice between the two depends on the specific requirements of the task at hand, such as the dataset size, feature space, and the desired balance between speed and accuracy. By leveraging the strengths of XGBoost and LightGBM, data scientists can develop highly accurate and efficient predictive models for a wide range of applications across various industries.

Chapter 17: Deep Learning Fundamentals

1. Neural Networks: Architecture and Layers

Neural Networks, inspired by the human brain's neural structure, are a powerful class of machine learning models that have revolutionized the field of artificial intelligence. These networks can learn complex patterns from data and make accurate predictions, enabling applications in computer vision, natural language processing, robotics, and more. In this comprehensive guide, we will delve into the architecture and layers of neural networks, exploring their fundamental principles, types, and applications.

A. Neural Network Architecture: Understanding the Basics

The architecture of a neural network refers to its structure or layout, including the number and arrangement of neurons (nodes) and layers. At its core, a neural network consists of an input layer, one or more hidden layers, and an output layer. Information flows through the network, passing from the input layer through the hidden layers to the output layer.

Each neuron in a neural network receives inputs from the previous layer and applies a transformation to produce an output, which is then passed to the next layer. The strength of the connections between neurons is represented by weights, and biases are introduced to control the neuron's activation function.

B. Neural Network Layers: Building Blocks of Learning

The layers of a neural network play a critical role in its ability to learn and generalize from the data. The most common types of layers found in neural networks include:

- **a. *Input Layer:*** The input layer is responsible for accepting the raw data and passing it forward to the first hidden layer. Each neuron in the input layer represents a feature or dimension of the input data.

b. Hidden Layers: Hidden layers are the intermediate layers between the input and output layers. They are responsible for learning and extracting patterns from the data. The number of hidden layers and the number of neurons in each layer are crucial factors that influence the network's capacity to learn complex representations.

c. Output Layer: The output layer produces the final predictions or results of the neural network. The number of neurons in the output layer depends on the type of task the network is designed for. For example, a binary classification task requires one neuron, while a multi-class classification task requires multiple neurons.

C. Common Types of Layers in Neural Networks

While the basic architecture remains the same, neural networks can be customized with different types of layers, each serving specific purposes. Some common types of layers include:

a. Fully Connected (Dense) Layer: In a fully connected layer, each neuron is connected to every neuron in the previous layer and vice versa. This type of layer is widely used in traditional feedforward neural networks.

b. Convolutional Layer: Convolutional layers are the building blocks of Convolutional Neural Networks (CNNs), a powerful architecture for image and video-related tasks. These layers apply convolutional filters to extract spatial patterns from the input data, allowing the network to capture local features.

c. *Recurrent Layer:* Recurrent Neural Networks (RNNs) contain recurrent layers, where the output of a neuron is fed back as an input to the same neuron in the next time step. RNNs are well-suited for sequential data and time-series prediction tasks.

d. *Pooling Layer:* Pooling layers reduce the spatial dimensions of the data, thereby decreasing the computational complexity and preventing overfitting. Max pooling and average pooling are common types of pooling operations.

e. *Batch Normalization Layer:* Batch normalization is a technique used to improve the training stability and speed of neural networks. It normalizes the inputs of a layer, making the optimization process more efficient.

f. Dropout Layer: Dropout is a regularization technique used to prevent overfitting in deep neural networks. During training, certain neurons are randomly dropped or set to zero with a certain probability, forcing the network to rely on other neurons and become more robust.

D. Understanding Deep Neural Networks

Deep Neural Networks (DNNs) refer to neural networks with multiple hidden layers. As the depth of the network increases, the capacity to learn complex representations improves. DNNs have the ability to automatically learn hierarchical features from the data, making them highly effective for tasks with large amounts of data and complex structures.

Deep learning has seen significant advancements in recent years, with the development of architectures like ResNet, DenseNet, and Transformer. These architectures have achieved state-of-the-art performance in various domains, such as image recognition, natural language processing, and speech recognition.

E. Applications of Neural Networks

Neural networks have found widespread applications across diverse fields:

a. ***Computer Vision:*** CNNs have demonstrated exceptional performance in image classification, object detection, segmentation, and style transfer tasks.

b. ***Natural Language Processing (NLP)***: Recurrent Neural Networks (RNNs) and Transformer-based architectures have significantly improved NLP tasks, including machine translation, sentiment analysis, and language generation.

c. ***Speech Recognition:*** Recurrent neural networks and attention-based models have achieved remarkable accuracy in speech recognition and language understanding.

d. ***Robotics and Autonomous Systems:*** Neural networks are used in robotics for tasks like robot control, navigation, and object manipulation.

e. ***Healthcare:*** Neural networks are employed for medical image analysis, disease diagnosis, and drug discovery.

F. Challenges and Future Directions

Despite their remarkable capabilities, neural networks still face some challenges. Training large networks with vast amounts of data requires substantial computational resources, and overfitting remains a concern. The interpretability of deep neural networks is also a subject of ongoing research.

In the future, advances in neural network architectures, regularization techniques, and optimization algorithms are expected to address these challenges. Research on explainable AI aims to make neural networks more interpretable, allowing us to understand their decision-making processes better.

Neural networks are a class of advanced machine learning techniques that have transformed the field of artificial intelligence. With their ability to learn complex patterns from data, they have achieved state-of-the-art performance in various domains, including computer vision, natural language processing, and robotics. Understanding the architecture and layers of neural networks enables data scientists and researchers to design powerful models tailored to specific tasks. As the field continues to progress, neural networks are likely to play an increasingly pivotal role in solving real-world problems and advancing our understanding of AI.

1. Activation Functions and Backpropagation

Activation functions and backpropagation are crucial components of neural networks, the foundation of modern advanced machine learning. Activation functions introduce non-linearity to the network, allowing it to learn complex relationships in the data, while backpropagation is the algorithm that enables the network to update its weights and improve its performance during training. In this comprehensive guide, we will delve into the concepts of activation functions and backpropagation, exploring their fundamental principles, types, and their vital role in the success of neural networks.

A. Activation Functions: Introducing Non-Linearity

In neural networks, an activation function is applied to each neuron's output to introduce non-linearity in the network. Without activation functions, the entire network would behave like a linear model, limiting its capacity to learn complex patterns from the data. The non-linearity introduced by activation functions allows the network to approximate highly nonlinear functions, making it capable of tackling intricate real-world problems.

- ***Types of Activation Functions:***

a. *Sigmoid Function*: The sigmoid function is one of the earliest activation functions used in neural networks. It squashes the output between 0 and 1, which is useful for binary classification tasks. However, it suffers from the vanishing gradient problem, which can slow down the training process in deep networks.

b. ReLU (Rectified Linear Unit): ReLU is a widely used activation function that sets negative values to zero and keeps positive values unchanged. ReLU's simplicity and ability to alleviate the vanishing gradient problem make it popular in deep learning.

c. ***Leaky ReLU:*** Leaky ReLU is a variation of ReLU that allows a small, non-zero gradient for negative inputs. This addresses the dying ReLU problem, where neurons can get stuck and stop learning during training.

d. ELU (Exponential Linear Unit): ELU is another activation function that introduces negative values for negative inputs, mitigating the dying ReLU problem. It has a smooth curve and can learn robust representations.

e. ***Swish Activation:*** Swish is a recently introduced activation function that shows promising performance. It combines the advantages of ReLU and Sigmoid, providing smoothness and non-linearity.

B. Backpropagation: Learning from Errors

Backpropagation, short for "backward propagation of errors," is the cornerstone of training neural networks. It is an optimization algorithm that enables the network to learn from its mistakes and update its weights to minimize the prediction errors. During the training process, the network's predictions are compared to the true labels, and the error is calculated using a loss function, such as Mean Squared Error (MSE) for regression tasks or Cross-Entropy Loss for classification tasks.

- ***Backpropagation Algorithm:***

a. Forward Pass: In the forward pass, the input data is passed through the network layer by layer, and the output is computed.

b. Loss Calculation: The difference between the predicted output and the true labels is calculated using the chosen loss function.

c. Backward Pass: During the backward pass, the error is propagated backward through the network. The gradients of the loss function with respect to the network's weights are computed using the chain rule of calculus.

d. Weight Update: The gradients obtained in the backward pass are used to update the network's weights using an optimization algorithm like

Stochastic Gradient Descent (SGD) or its variants.

e. ***Repeat:*** The forward and backward passes are repeated iteratively on batches of data until the network converges or reaches a predefined number of epochs.

C. Importance of Activation Functions and Backpropagation

Activation functions and backpropagation are vital for the success of neural networks:

a. ***Non-Linearity:*** Activation functions introduce non-linearity, allowing the network to learn complex relationships and approximate nonlinear functions.

b. ***Learning from Errors:*** Backpropagation enables the network to learn from its mistakes by updating the weights based on the prediction errors.

c. *Deep Learning:* The combination of activation functions and backpropagation is the foundation of deep learning, enabling the successful training of large and complex neural networks.

d. *Universal Approximation Theorem:* Activation functions, along with a sufficient number of neurons and layers, enable neural networks to approximate any continuous function, as proven by the Universal Approximation Theorem.

D. Challenges and Considerations

While activation functions and backpropagation are powerful tools, they come with some challenges:

a. *Vanishing Gradient Problem:* Some activation functions, like the sigmoid function, suffer from vanishing gradients, making the training process slow and challenging in deep networks.

b. Choosing the Right Activation Function: Selecting the appropriate activation function depends on the nature of the problem and the characteristics of the data. Experimentation and tuning are often required to find the optimal activation function.

c. Overfitting: Neural networks are susceptible to overfitting, especially when they have many layers and parameters. Regularization techniques, such as dropout, are used to combat overfitting.

E. Applications of Activation Functions and Backpropagation

Activation functions and backpropagation have enabled the success of neural networks in various applications:

a. *Computer Vision:* Neural networks with ReLU activation are commonly used in computer vision tasks like image classification and object detection.

b. *Natural Language Processing (NLP):* Recurrent Neural Networks (RNNs) with appropriate activation functions are widely used in NLP for tasks like machine translation and sentiment analysis.

c. *Speech Recognition:* Deep neural networks with specialized activation functions are employed in speech recognition systems.

d. *Autonomous Systems:* Neural networks are used in autonomous systems like self-driving cars for perception and decision-making.

Activation functions and backpropagation are fundamental components of neural networks, responsible for their ability to learn complex patterns from data and make accurate predictions. The choice of activation function can significantly impact the network's performance, and backpropagation is the key to optimizing the network's weights during training. As neural networks continue to advance, researchers are exploring new activation functions and optimization algorithms to further improve their capabilities. Understanding these essential concepts empowers data scientists and machine learning practitioners to design and train efficient and powerful neural networks for a wide range of applications across various industries.

1. Loss Functions for Neural Networks

Loss functions play a pivotal role in training neural networks by quantifying the difference between the predicted outputs and the actual target values. They serve as optimization objectives, guiding the network's weights and biases towards the most accurate predictions. Selecting an appropriate loss function is crucial, as it depends on the nature of the problem, the type of data, and the desired outcome. In this comprehensive guide, we will delve into the concepts of loss functions for neural networks, exploring their fundamental principles, types, and applications.

A. Understanding Loss Functions in Neural Networks

In neural networks, the primary objective during training is to minimize the loss function. The loss function measures the discrepancy between the predicted outputs and the true target values, quantifying the model's performance on the training data. The goal is to find the set of weights and biases that minimize the loss function, leading to accurate predictions on unseen data.

B. Types of Loss Functions

There are various types of loss functions used in neural networks, each suited for specific tasks:

a. Mean Squared Error (MSE): MSE is a popular loss function used for regression tasks, where the predicted outputs are continuous numerical values. It calculates the average squared difference between the predicted values and the true target values. MSE is sensitive to outliers and penalizes large prediction errors heavily.

b. Mean Absolute Error (MAE): MAE is another loss function used for regression tasks. It calculates the average absolute difference between the predicted values and the true target values. MAE is less sensitive to outliers compared to MSE.

c. *Binary Cross-Entropy (Log Loss):* Binary cross-entropy is commonly used for binary classification tasks. It measures the dissimilarity between the predicted probabilities and the true binary labels. Cross-entropy loss is suitable when dealing with imbalanced datasets.

d. Categorical Cross-Entropy: Categorical cross-entropy is used for multi-class classification tasks. It measures the difference between the predicted class probabilities and the true one-hot encoded labels.

e. *Sparse Categorical Cross-Entropy:* Sparse categorical cross-entropy is similar to categorical cross-entropy but is used when the true labels are represented as integers rather than one-hot encoded vectors.

f. Hinge Loss (SVM Loss): Hinge loss is typically used for Support Vector Machine (SVM) classifiers but can also be used for binary classification in neural networks. It aims to maximize the margin between the decision boundary and the data points.

g. Kullback-Leibler Divergence (KL Divergence): KL divergence is a measure of dissimilarity between two probability distributions. It is often used in probabilistic models and generative models like Variational Autoencoders (VAEs).

C. Choosing the Right Loss Function

Selecting the appropriate loss function depends on the task and the characteristics of the data. Some considerations include:

a. ***Task Type:*** Regression tasks require loss functions like MSE or MAE, while binary classification tasks use binary cross-entropy. For multi-class classification, categorical cross-entropy or sparse categorical cross-entropy is appropriate.

b. ***Data Distribution:*** The choice of loss function may also be influenced by the data distribution. For example, if the dataset is imbalanced, cross-entropy loss is preferred over accuracy for binary classification.

c. ***Network Architecture:*** Certain loss functions are more compatible with specific network architectures. For example, cross-entropy loss is commonly used with softmax activation in the output layer for multi-class classification.

D. Handling Imbalanced Data with Custom Loss Functions

In cases where the dataset is highly imbalanced, custom loss functions can be designed to address the imbalance issue. One approach is to modify the standard loss function to give more importance to minority class samples. Alternatively, focal loss and class-balanced loss are specialized techniques designed to tackle class imbalance problems in classification tasks.

E. Loss Functions for Advanced Applications

For more complex tasks and specialized applications, advanced loss functions are used:

a. *GAN Loss Functions:* In Generative Adversarial Networks (GANs), two loss functions are used - generator loss and discriminator loss – to optimize the generator and discriminator networks, respectively.

b. Triplet Loss: Triplet loss is used in tasks like face recognition and image retrieval, where the goal is to learn embeddings such that the distance between similar instances is minimized while the distance between dissimilar instances is maximized.

c. Siamese Loss: Siamese loss is used for one-shot learning tasks, where the goal is to learn representations for a pair of data points such that similar instances have lower distances in the learned feature space.

F. Multi-Objective Loss Functions

In some scenarios, it may be necessary to optimize multiple objectives simultaneously.

Multi-objective loss functions allow the network to optimize multiple criteria, striking a balance between conflicting objectives. These functions are useful in scenarios where the model's performance depends on multiple metrics, such as accuracy and fairness.

G. Regularization and Loss Functions

Regularization techniques, such as L1 and L2 regularization, can be incorporated into the loss function to prevent overfitting. Regularization adds a penalty term based on the weights, discouraging the model from relying too heavily on specific features or neurons.

H. Applications of Loss Functions

Loss functions are used in various machine learning tasks:

a. *Image Classification:* Cross-entropy loss is commonly used in image classification tasks to optimize the output probabilities for each class.

b. *Object Detection:* Loss functions like smooth L1 loss are used in object detection tasks to optimize bounding box predictions.

c. *Semantic Segmentation:* Dice loss and Jaccard loss are used for optimizing segmentation masks.

d. *Generative Models:* In generative models like VAEs and GANs, custom loss functions are used to optimize the generators and discriminators.

Loss functions are critical components of neural networks, guiding the optimization process during training. The choice of loss function depends on the task and the nature of the data. Understanding the different types of loss functions and their applications empowers data scientists and machine learning practitioners to design and train powerful models that deliver accurate predictions and solve complex real-world problems. The continuous exploration and development of novel loss functions will further advance the capabilities of neural networks, propelling the field of machine learning to new heights.

Chapter 18: Convolutional Neural Networks (CNNs) for Image Analysis

1. Understanding CNN Architecture

Convolutional Neural Networks (CNNs) have emerged as a groundbreaking technology in the field of machine learning and artificial intelligence. They have revolutionized various applications, including image and video recognition, natural language processing, and autonomous systems. In this comprehensive essay, we will delve into the fundamentals of CNN architecture, exploring the underlying concepts, components, and advanced techniques that have made CNNs so powerful and widely adopted.

A. Introduction to Convolutional Neural Networks:

Convolutional Neural Networks, inspired by the human visual system, are a class of deep neural networks designed to process and recognize visual data efficiently. Traditional neural networks lack the ability to handle spatial relationships and have a high computational cost when dealing with image data due to the sheer volume of parameters. CNNs overcome these limitations by utilizing convolutional layers that perform localized and shared parameter operations, making them particularly suitable for image-related tasks.

A. Key Components of CNN Architecture:

A typical CNN architecture consists of several key components:

a) Convolutional Layers: These layers are the core building blocks of CNNs. They consist of learnable filters (kernels) that slide over the input data and perform element-wise multiplication followed by summation. This operation helps in detecting specific patterns and features within the input, effectively capturing hierarchical representations.

b) Activation Functions: After the convolution operation, an activation function is applied element-wise to introduce non-linearity in the network. ReLU (Rectified Linear Unit) is one of the commonly used activation functions, which helps in mitigating the vanishing gradient problem and accelerating the training process.

c) Pooling Layers: Pooling layers are utilized to downsample the spatial dimensions of the feature maps, reducing computational complexity and making the network more robust to variations in the input. Max-pooling and average-pooling are popular techniques used for this purpose.

d) Fully Connected Layers: Following several convolutional and pooling layers, fully connected layers are employed to make predictions or perform classification tasks. These layers connect every neuron from the previous layer to every neuron in the subsequent layer, enabling high-level feature extraction and decision-making.

A. *Advanced Techniques in CNN Architecture:*

Over time, researchers have introduced various advanced techniques to enhance the performance and efficiency of CNNs. Some of the notable techniques are:

a) Transfer Learning: Transfer learning is a powerful approach that leverages pre-trained models on large-scale datasets and adapts them to specific tasks with limited data. By fine-tuning the pre-trained models, CNNs can achieve state-of-the-art performance even with a smaller dataset.

b) Batch Normalization: Batch normalization is a technique that normalizes the activations of each layer to have zero mean and unit variance during training. This helps in stabilizing and accelerating the training process, leading to faster convergence and better generalization.

c) Dropout: Dropout is a regularization technique used to prevent overfitting in deep neural networks, including CNNs. During training, random neurons are "dropped out," meaning they are temporarily excluded from the network, encouraging the remaining neurons to become more robust and independent.

d) Data Augmentation: Data augmentation involves applying random transformations (e.g., rotations, flips, and translations) to the training data, effectively increasing the diversity of the dataset. This augmentation helps the model generalize better and reduces the risk of overfitting.

A. CNN Architectures and Applications:

The success of CNNs can be attributed, in part, to the development of various powerful CNN architectures tailored to specific tasks. Some popular CNN architectures include:

a) AlexNet: One of the pioneering CNN architectures, AlexNet, introduced in 2012, demonstrated the potential of deep learning in image recognition tasks. Its design included multiple convolutional and pooling layers and helped pave the way for more sophisticated networks.

b) VGGNet: VGGNet, proposed in 2014, is known for its uniform architecture, consisting of multiple layers with small-sized kernels. Despite being computationally expensive, VGGNet achieved state-of-the-art results on image recognition challenges and inspired later architectures.

c) ResNet: Residual Network (ResNet) is a groundbreaking architecture that introduced the concept of residual connections. ResNet blocks enable the training of very deep networks by mitigating the vanishing gradient problem, leading to significantly improved performance.

d) Inception (GoogLeNet): Inception, also known as GoogLeNet, proposed an innovative "Inception module" that used multiple filter sizes within the same layer. This approach allowed the network to capture features at various scales and achieved high accuracy while being computationally efficient.

e) Transformers: Originally introduced for natural language processing tasks, Transformers have also found application in computer vision tasks. The self-attention mechanism in Transformers enables capturing global dependencies between image elements, leading to state-of-the-art performance in tasks like image captioning and object detection.

A. Future Directions:

The field of CNN architecture continues to evolve rapidly, and researchers are exploring exciting avenues to further improve these models. Some potential future directions include:

a) Attention Mechanisms: Incorporating attention mechanisms into CNN architectures can enable more adaptive and context-aware feature extraction, potentially improving performance in tasks involving fine-grained details.

b) Explainability and Interpretability: As CNNs are increasingly used in critical applications such as healthcare and autonomous systems, research on making CNNs more interpretable and explainable is gaining importance to enhance transparency and trustworthiness.

c) Few-Shot Learning: Addressing the challenge of learning from limited data remains a key area of interest. Techniques that enable CNNs to learn from small or even single-shot examples could have significant implications for practical applications.

In conclusion, Convolutional Neural Networks (CNNs) have become a cornerstone of modern machine learning and artificial intelligence, especially in image and video-related tasks. Through their unique architecture, consisting of convolutional layers, activation functions, pooling layers, and fully connected layers, CNNs can efficiently process visual data and extract meaningful features. The introduction of advanced techniques such as transfer learning, batch normalization, dropout, and data augmentation has further boosted their performance and generalization capabilities. As CNN architecture continues to evolve and find novel applications, the future holds promising developments that can potentially push the boundaries of AI and lead to even more remarkable achievements in various domains.

1. Image Recognition and Classification with CNNs

Image recognition and classification are fundamental problems in the field of computer vision, with numerous real-world applications ranging from autonomous vehicles to medical imaging and content-based image retrieval. Convolutional Neural Networks (CNNs) have emerged as the go-to technique for solving these tasks due to their exceptional ability to extract hierarchical and meaningful features from images. In this comprehensive essay, we will delve into the intricacies of image recognition and classification with CNNs, exploring the underlying principles, advanced techniques, and insights that have made CNNs the state-of-the-art approach for visual tasks.

A. *Introduction to Image Recognition and Classification:*

Image recognition and classification involve the process of automatically identifying objects or patterns within digital images and assigning them to predefined categories or classes. This task is challenging due to the complexity and high dimensionality of image data. Traditional image processing techniques often rely on hand-crafted features, which may not be optimal for capturing intricate patterns and variations in images. CNNs address this limitation by learning features directly from the data, making them more flexible and powerful in handling various image recognition and classification tasks.

A. The Role of Convolutional Neural Networks (CNNs) in Image Tasks:

CNNs have revolutionized the field of computer vision by significantly improving the accuracy and efficiency of image recognition and classification tasks. The architecture of CNNs is inspired by the visual cortex of the human brain, where neurons respond to specific regions of the visual field. Similarly, the layers of a CNN are designed to detect specific patterns, edges, and textures in localized regions of an image. By combining multiple convolutional and pooling layers, CNNs can learn complex hierarchical representations that are crucial for accurate classification.

A. Key Components of CNNs for Image Recognition:

A CNN architecture for image recognition and classification consists of several essential components:

a) Convolutional Layers: These layers use learnable filters (kernels) to slide over the input image, extracting local features through convolutional operations. The filters capture patterns such as edges, corners, and textures, gradually building higher-level features in deeper layers.

b) Activation Functions: After the convolutional operation, an activation function, such as ReLU (Rectified Linear Unit), introduces non-linearity to the network. ReLU activation has become popular due to its computational efficiency and the ability to alleviate the vanishing gradient problem.

c) Pooling Layers: Pooling layers downsample the feature maps generated by the convolutional layers. Max-pooling and average-pooling are commonly used techniques, helping to reduce the spatial dimensions while preserving essential features and making the network more computationally efficient.

d) Fully Connected Layers: Following several convolutional and pooling layers, fully connected layers are used to perform high-level feature extraction and decision-making. The output of these layers is typically fed into a softmax function for probability distribution across different classes, enabling the final classification.

A. Advanced Techniques for Improved Image Recognition:

Several advanced techniques have been introduced to enhance the performance and robustness of CNNs for image recognition and classification tasks:

a) Transfer Learning: Transfer learning is a powerful approach where a pre-trained CNN model on a large dataset, such as ImageNet, is fine-tuned for a specific task with limited labeled data. This technique leverages the knowledge and feature representations learned from the vast dataset, allowing the model to perform well even with smaller datasets.

b) Data Augmentation: Data augmentation involves applying various transformations to the training data, such as rotations, flips, and translations. This technique increases the diversity of the dataset, reducing overfitting and enhancing the model's generalization capabilities.

c) Batch Normalization: Batch normalization normalizes the activations of each layer during training, making the optimization process more stable and accelerating convergence. This technique has proven to be effective in deeper CNN architectures, reducing training time and improving performance.

d) Dropout: Dropout is a regularization technique used to prevent overfitting by randomly deactivating neurons during training. This encourages the network to be more robust and prevents it from relying too heavily on specific neurons.

A. Applications of CNNs in Image Recognition and Classification:

CNNs have demonstrated exceptional performance in various image recognition and classification tasks, enabling advancements in several domains:

a) Object Detection: CNNs are used in object detection tasks to not only classify objects but also localize their positions within the image.

Region-based CNNs and single-stage detectors, such as YOLO (You Only Look Once) and SSD (Single Shot Multibox Detector), have achieved remarkable results in real-time object detection.

b) Image Segmentation: CNNs are employed in image segmentation tasks to partition an image into meaningful segments or regions. Techniques like U-Net and FCN (Fully Convolutional Network) have been successful in medical image segmentation and semantic segmentation tasks.

c) Image Captioning: CNNs combined with Recurrent Neural Networks (RNNs) are used for generating descriptive captions for images. These models learn to encode the visual content of an image and then generate corresponding captions.

d) Facial Recognition: CNNs are widely used in facial recognition systems, identifying individuals based on facial features. FaceNet and VGG-Face are notable examples of CNN architectures used for face recognition.

A. Challenges and Future Directions:

While CNNs have achieved impressive results in image recognition and classification tasks, several challenges and future research directions remain:

a) Adversarial Attacks: CNNs are susceptible to adversarial attacks, where small perturbations to an input image can lead to misclassification. Developing robust CNN architectures to mitigate these attacks is an ongoing challenge.

b) Interpretability and Explainability: CNNs are often treated as black-box models, lacking transparency in their decision-making process. Research on understanding and interpreting CNN decisions is essential for building trust in AI systems.

c) Handling Limited Data: Training CNNs with limited labeled data remains a challenge. Few-shot and zero-shot learning techniques aim to address this issue, enabling CNNs to learn from scarce data effectively.

d) Continual Learning: Continual learning focuses on enabling CNNs to learn from a continuous stream of data, adapting to new classes without forgetting previously learned knowledge.

In conclusion, CNNs have revolutionized image recognition and classification tasks, leveraging their hierarchical feature extraction capabilities to achieve remarkable performance in various computer vision applications. Their ability to automatically learn meaningful representations from raw image data, combined with advanced techniques like transfer learning, data augmentation, batch normalization, and dropout, has made CNNs the state-of-the-art approach in the field. As researchers continue to tackle challenges and explore future directions, CNNs are expected to play an increasingly vital role in shaping the future of AI, with widespread applications across industries and domains.

1. Transfer Learning and Fine-Tuning

Transfer learning and fine-tuning are advanced machine learning techniques that have revolutionized the field of deep learning, particularly in the context of Convolutional Neural Networks (CNNs). These techniques address the challenges of limited data and computationally expensive model training by leveraging pre-trained models and adapting them to new tasks. In this comprehensive essay, we will delve into the concepts of transfer learning and fine-tuning, exploring their underlying principles, applications, benefits, and insightful considerations for their successful implementation.

A. Introduction to Transfer Learning:

Transfer learning is a machine learning paradigm that involves transferring knowledge from one task or domain to another. In the context of deep learning, it refers to using pre-trained neural network models, typically trained on large-scale datasets, to perform well on related but different tasks with smaller datasets. The fundamental idea behind transfer learning is that the knowledge learned from one task can be transferred and utilized to enhance the learning and generalization of a different but related task.

A. Principles of Transfer Learning:

Transfer learning relies on the intuition that lower layers of a deep neural network capture general and low-level features, such as edges and textures, that are applicable across various tasks. As we move to higher layers in the network, the features become more specific and task-dependent. By reusing the lower layers of a pre-trained model and replacing the top layers with new task-specific layers, we can leverage the pre-learned features to expedite the training and improve the performance of the model on the new task.

A. Benefits of Transfer Learning:

Transfer learning offers several key advantages, making it an attractive approach for various machine learning scenarios:

a) ***Reduced Training Time:*** Since transfer learning reuses pre-trained layers, it significantly reduces the training time required for the model. The lower layers, which capture general features, no longer need to be trained from scratch, saving computational resources and time.

b) ***Improved Generalization:*** By leveraging knowledge from a related task, the model starts with a more robust representation, leading to improved generalization and better performance on the new task, especially when the target task has limited training data.

c) Handling Limited Data: In scenarios where acquiring a large labeled dataset is challenging or expensive, transfer learning proves to be highly effective, as it allows models to perform well with smaller datasets.

A. Process of Transfer Learning:

The process of transfer learning typically involves the following steps:

a) Pre-training: The first step is to train a deep neural network on a large-scale dataset, often from a different but related domain. This pre-trained model is referred to as the "base model."

b) Feature Extraction: After pre-training, the lower layers of the base model, which capture general features, are retained. The last few layers, known as the "top layers," are discarded or replaced with new layers to suit the target task.

c) Fine-Tuning: The new task-specific layers are then added on top of the retained base model. The model is then fine-tuned by training it on the new task's dataset. During fine-tuning, the weights of the lower layers are often frozen to preserve the pre-learned features, while the top layers' weights are updated to adapt to the new task.

A. Fine-Tuning in Transfer Learning:

Fine-tuning is a critical aspect of transfer learning, as it allows the model to adapt and specialize in the new task while retaining the knowledge gained from the pre-training phase. The process of fine-tuning involves:

a) Choosing Layers to Fine-Tune: Depending on the size of the new dataset and the similarity between the base and target tasks, different strategies can be employed. Generally, the top layers of the base model are fine-tuned since they are more task-specific, while the lower layers are frozen to retain their generic feature representations.

b) Learning Rate Scheduling: During fine-tuning, it is common to use a lower learning rate to avoid drastically changing the pre-learned weights. This helps in stabilizing the training process and preventing catastrophic forgetting of the knowledge gained from pre-training.

c) Balancing the Fine-Tuning Process: Fine-tuning requires finding the right balance between adapting the model to the new task and preserving the valuable knowledge from pre-training. This balance is often achieved through experimentation and tuning hyperparameters.

A. Applications of Transfer Learning and Fine-Tuning:

Transfer learning and fine-tuning have found numerous applications across various domains and have led to significant advancements in the field of deep learning. Some notable applications include:

a) Image Recognition: Pre-trained CNN models, such as VGG, ResNet, and Inception, have been fine-tuned for specific image recognition tasks, achieving state-of-the-art results with limited training data.

b) Natural Language Processing: Pre-trained language models like BERT (Bidirectional Encoder Representations from Transformers) have been fine-tuned for tasks like sentiment analysis, named entity recognition, and question-answering, showcasing the power of transfer learning in NLP.

c) Medical Imaging: Transfer learning has shown promise in medical imaging tasks, where limited annotated data is a common challenge. Pre-trained CNN models are adapted and fine-tuned for tasks like disease classification, lesion detection, and organ segmentation.

d) Autonomous Systems: Transfer learning and fine-tuning have been instrumental in training deep learning models for autonomous vehicles, where models trained on large-scale datasets can be adapted to specific road conditions and environments.

A. Considerations and Challenges:

While transfer learning and fine-tuning offer numerous benefits, several considerations and challenges need to be taken into account:

a) Domain Shift: Transfer learning assumes that the source and target tasks share some degree of similarity. If the domains are vastly different, the transfer may not be effective, leading to degraded performance.

b) Overfitting: Fine-tuning on a small dataset can lead to overfitting. Employing regularization techniques like dropout and data augmentation can help mitigate this issue.

c) Task Selection: Choosing an appropriate pre-trained model and task for transfer learning is crucial. An unrelated or mismatched source task may not provide significant benefits for the target task.

d) Ethical Concerns: Fine-tuning pre-trained models for specific tasks raises ethical considerations, especially when dealing with sensitive or biased data. Careful examination and mitigation of biases are essential to avoid unintended consequences.

Transfer learning and fine-tuning have emerged as indispensable tools in the field of deep learning, enabling models to leverage knowledge from pre-trained models and adapt to new tasks with limited data. These techniques have revolutionized various applications, including image recognition, natural language processing, and medical imaging. By combining the power of pre-trained models with fine-tuning strategies, transfer learning has opened up new possibilities in AI research and practical applications. As researchers continue to refine these techniques and address challenges, the future holds promising advancements that will further elevate the capabilities of deep learning models across diverse domains.

Chapter 19: Recurrent Neural Networks (RNNs) for Sequence Data

1. Introduction to RNNs and LSTM

Recurrent Neural Networks (RNNs) and Long Short-Term Memory (LSTM) networks are powerful and versatile deep learning techniques that have revolutionized sequence modeling and prediction tasks. Unlike traditional feedforward neural networks, RNNs and LSTMs can process sequential data, such as time series, natural language, and audio, by maintaining hidden states that capture temporal dependencies. In this comprehensive essay, we will explore the fundamentals of RNNs and LSTM networks, their underlying principles, applications, and the advantages they bring to advanced machine learning tasks.

A. Introduction to Recurrent Neural Networks (RNNs):

Recurrent Neural Networks are a class of neural networks designed to process sequential data by maintaining hidden states that capture the temporal information of the input sequence. Unlike feedforward neural networks, RNNs have loops in their architecture, allowing information to persist and be shared across time steps. This recurrence property enables RNNs to model sequences of arbitrary lengths, making them suitable for tasks like natural language processing, speech recognition, and time series analysis.

A. Principles of RNNs:

The key principle behind RNNs lies in their ability to maintain hidden states that encode past information and influence future predictions. At each time step t, an RNN takes an input vector x_t and the hidden state h_{t-1} from the previous time step. The input and the previous hidden state are combined to compute a new hidden state h_t, which acts as a memory of past information. The current hidden state h_t is then used to generate the output at the current time step or as an input for the next time step.

A. Challenges of Basic RNNs:

While RNNs are powerful in capturing sequential dependencies, they suffer from the vanishing gradient problem, which hinders long-term memory retention during training. As the RNN is unrolled through time during backpropagation, gradients can become very small, leading to difficulties in learning long-range dependencies. This limitation limits the effectiveness of basic RNNs in tasks requiring extended temporal context.

A. ***Introduction to Long Short-Term Memory (LSTM) Networks:***

Long Short-Term Memory (LSTM) networks are a variant of RNNs designed to address the vanishing gradient problem and effectively capture long-term dependencies in sequential data. LSTMs were introduced to overcome the limitations of basic RNNs and have become a standard choice for various time-series and natural language processing tasks.

A. ***Principles of LSTM Networks:***

LSTM networks maintain a more sophisticated memory cell that can selectively retain and forget information over multiple time steps. The LSTM cell consists of three main components: an input gate, a forget gate, and an output gate. These gates are responsible for controlling the flow of information in and out of the memory cell, allowing LSTMs to learn long-term dependencies while mitigating the vanishing gradient problem.

A. The LSTM Memory Cell:

At each time step t, the LSTM cell receives an input x_t and the previous hidden state h_{t-1}. The input and hidden state are combined, and the input gate decides which information from the input to store in the cell's memory. The forget gate determines which information to discard from the previous cell state c_{t-1}, effectively controlling the retention of long-term dependencies. The output gate regulates the output at the current time step, which is a combination of the current cell state c_t and the hidden state h_t.

A. Advantages of LSTM Networks:

LSTM networks offer several key advantages over basic RNNs:

a) Capturing Long-Term Dependencies: The LSTM memory cell's design enables the network to learn and retain long-term dependencies, making it effective in tasks that require an extended temporal context.

b) Mitigating Vanishing Gradient Problem: The gating mechanisms in LSTMs allow them to propagate gradients effectively during training, mitigating the vanishing gradient problem and enabling more stable and efficient learning.

c) Versatility in Sequence Tasks: LSTMs can handle sequences of varying lengths, making them versatile for tasks like speech recognition, machine translation, sentiment analysis, and music generation.

A. Applications of RNNs and LSTMs:

RNNs and LSTMs have found extensive applications in various domains, transforming the way sequential data is modeled and analyzed:

a) Natural Language Processing: In NLP, LSTMs are used for tasks such as language modeling, sentiment analysis, machine translation, and text generation. They excel in understanding the contextual meaning of words in sentences and maintaining long-range dependencies in the text.

b) Speech Recognition: RNNs and LSTMs have shown remarkable performance in automatic speech recognition (ASR) systems, converting audio signals into transcriptions. They can capture the temporal patterns and phonetic information essential for accurate speech recognition.

c) Time Series Analysis: RNNs are widely used for time series forecasting, anomaly detection, and stock price prediction. LSTMs, in particular, are well-suited for modeling long-term dependencies in time series data, leading to improved predictions.

d) Music Generation: LSTM-based models have been utilized for music generation tasks, where the network learns the patterns and structure of music and composes new musical pieces.

A. *Considerations and Challenges:*

While RNNs and LSTMs offer powerful capabilities, there are several considerations and challenges to keep in mind:

a) Computational Complexity: LSTMs can be computationally expensive, especially for longer sequences and large vocabularies. Model optimization and hardware accelerators may be required for efficient training.

b) Overfitting: Like any deep learning model, RNNs and LSTMs are prone to overfitting, especially when dealing with small datasets. Regularization techniques, such as dropout and weight decay, can be used to address this issue.

c) Hyperparameter Tuning: Selecting the appropriate architecture and hyperparameters for RNNs and LSTMs can significantly impact their performance. Careful experimentation and tuning are necessary for optimal results.

RNNs and LSTMs are foundational techniques in the field of deep learning, enabling the effective modeling and analysis of sequential data. While RNNs capture temporal dependencies, LSTMs have emerged as a powerful variant that addresses the vanishing gradient problem and captures long-term dependencies. Their versatility and application in natural language processing, speech recognition, time series analysis, and music generation have led to significant advancements in various domains. As researchers continue to explore new architectural improvements and tackle challenges, RNNs and LSTMs will remain at the forefront of advanced machine learning techniques, shaping the future of sequence modeling and prediction tasks.

1. Text Generation with RNNs

Text generation is an exciting and challenging task in the field of natural language processing (NLP), where the goal is to create coherent and meaningful text that resembles human-written language. Recurrent Neural Networks (RNNs) have emerged as a powerful and popular choice for text generation due to their ability to model sequential data and capture contextual dependencies. In this comprehensive essay, we will delve into the fundamentals of text generation with RNNs, exploring the underlying principles, techniques, applications, and insightful considerations for successful text generation.

A. Introduction to Text Generation:

Text generation involves automatically creating new text that exhibits coherence and semantic meaning. This task is essential in various applications, such as chatbots, language translation, creative writing, and data augmentation for training language models. Unlike traditional rule-based approaches, deep learning techniques like RNNs have shown promising results in generating high-quality text that resembles human language.

A. Recurrent Neural Networks (RNNs) for Text Generation:

RNNs are a class of neural networks designed to process sequential data, making them well-suited for text generation tasks. The architecture of RNNs includes recurrent connections that allow information to persist and be shared across time steps. This property enables RNNs to maintain context and dependencies in the generated text, resulting in more coherent and contextually appropriate language.

A. ***Principles of Text Generation with RNNs:***

The fundamental principle behind text generation with RNNs lies in the sequential nature of language. At each time step, an RNN takes an input token, such as a word or character, and processes it along with the hidden state from the previous time step. The current hidden state represents the contextual information up to that point in the text. This process is repeated for each subsequent token in the generated text, allowing the model to capture dependencies and generate meaningful sequences.

A. ***Training RNNs for Text Generation:***

To train RNNs for text generation, a large corpus of text is used as the training dataset. The text is tokenized into individual words or characters, and the RNN is trained to predict the next token in the sequence given the previous tokens and hidden state. This training process involves optimizing the model's parameters to minimize the difference between predicted and actual tokens.

A. Challenges in Text Generation:

Text generation poses several challenges that need to be addressed for successful results:

a) Coherence and Context: Ensuring that the generated text is coherent and contextually appropriate remains a challenge, as RNNs tend to rely heavily on the immediate context and may struggle with long-range dependencies.

b) Diversity and Creativity: Generating diverse and creative text is essential to avoid repetitive or monotonous outputs. Balancing between generating novel text and staying coherent with the context is a challenging task.

c) Evaluation Metrics: Measuring the quality of generated text is subjective and challenging. Traditional evaluation metrics may not fully capture the richness and creativity of human language.

A. Techniques for Improved Text Generation:

Several advanced techniques have been proposed to enhance the quality and creativity of text generation with RNNs:

a) Teacher Forcing: During training, teacher forcing involves feeding the true tokens as inputs to the RNN instead of using the model's predictions. This approach stabilizes training but may lead to a discrepancy between training and inference, where the model struggles to handle its own generated text.

b) Beam Search: During inference, beam search is used to explore multiple potential sequences of tokens and find the most likely one based on a scoring criterion. Beam search promotes diversity in the generated text and improves the overall quality of the output.

c) Temperature Sampling: Temperature sampling is a technique that controls the randomness of the generated text. By adjusting the temperature parameter, the model can be forced to generate more conservative or more diverse text.

d) Attention Mechanism: Attention mechanisms enhance text generation by allowing the model to focus on different parts of the input text during the generation process. This helps address the issue of long-range dependencies and improves coherence.

A. Applications of Text Generation with RNNs:

Text generation with RNNs finds numerous applications across various domains, showcasing the versatility and potential of this technique:

a) Chatbots and Conversational Agents: RNN-based text generation is used to build conversational agents and chatbots capable of engaging in human-like interactions.

b) Language Translation: RNNs can be used to generate translated text in language translation tasks, where they convert text from one language to another.

c) Story Generation and Creative Writing: Text generation models are employed to produce creative writing, such as storytelling, poetry, and song lyrics.

d) Data Augmentation: Text generation is utilized for data augmentation in NLP tasks, where synthetic data is generated to increase the size of the training dataset and improve model performance.

A. *Ethical Considerations in Text Generation:*

Text generation with RNNs raises ethical considerations, especially when it comes to generating human-like text. There is a risk of generating biased or harmful content, and ensuring responsible use of such technology is crucial. Ethical guidelines and filters are necessary to prevent misuse and promote responsible AI practices.

A. *Future Directions in Text Generation:*

The field of text generation with RNNs is continuously evolving, and researchers are exploring exciting directions to address challenges and improve performance:

a) GANs for Text Generation: Generative Adversarial Networks (GANs) are being explored for text generation, where a generator model is trained to produce text that is then evaluated by a discriminator model. This adversarial setup aims to generate more realistic and diverse text.

b) Controllable Text Generation: Research is ongoing to develop methods for controlling the style, sentiment, or other attributes of the generated text, allowing users to specify desired characteristics in the output.

c) Multimodal Text Generation: Combining text generation with other modalities, such as images or audio, opens up new possibilities for generating rich and interactive content.

Text generation with RNNs is a fascinating and rapidly evolving area of research in the field of natural language processing. RNNs' ability to model sequential data and capture dependencies makes them well-suited for generating coherent and meaningful text. Advanced techniques such as teacher forcing, beam search, attention mechanisms, and temperature sampling have improved the quality and creativity of generated text. The applications of text generation are diverse, ranging from chatbots and language translation to creative writing and data augmentation. However, ethical considerations and responsible use of this technology are vital to address potential challenges and ensure positive outcomes. As researchers continue to innovate and explore new directions, text generation with RNNs is expected to play a significant role in shaping the future of human-computer interactions and creative content generation.

1. Sequence-to-Sequence Models for Language Translation

Sequence-to-Sequence (Seq2Seq) models have revolutionized the field of natural language processing (NLP), particularly in language translation tasks. These advanced machine learning techniques enable the automatic translation of text from one language to another, making them indispensable in a multilingual world. In this comprehensive essay, we will explore the fundamentals of Seq2Seq models for language translation, including their underlying principles, architecture, training process, applications, and insightful considerations for successful implementation.

A. Introduction to Sequence-to-Sequence

Models:

Sequence-to-Sequence models, introduced by Sutskever et al. in 2014, are a class of neural network architectures designed to process sequences of arbitrary lengths and map one sequence to another. This paradigm is particularly relevant for language translation, where the goal is to take a sequence of text in one language (source language) and generate the corresponding translation in another language (target language).

A. Architecture of Sequence-to-Sequence Models:

Seq2Seq models consist of two main components: an encoder and a decoder. The encoder processes the input sequence and generates a fixed-length vector representation, capturing the contextual information of the input text. This vector, often referred to as the "context vector" or "thought vector," serves as the initial hidden state for the decoder. The decoder then uses this context vector to generate the output sequence in the target language.

A. ***Encoder in Sequence-to-Sequence Models:***

The encoder of a Seq2Seq model typically employs a Recurrent Neural Network (RNN) or a Long Short-Term Memory (LSTM) network to process the input sequence. At each time step, the encoder takes an input token (e.g., a word) and updates its hidden state based on the input token and the previous hidden state. This process continues until the entire input sequence is processed, and the final hidden state represents the contextual information of the entire sequence.

A. ***Decoder in Sequence-to-Sequence Models:***

The decoder of a Seq2Seq model is also an RNN or LSTM, designed to generate the output sequence in the target language. At each time step, the decoder takes the context vector (generated by the encoder) and the previous hidden state as inputs. It then updates its hidden state based on these inputs and generates an output token (e.g., a word) representing the translated text. The process continues until an end-of-sequence token is generated, indicating the completion of the translation.

A. ***Training Sequence-to-Sequence***

Models:

Training Seq2Seq models for language translation involves a process known as teacher forcing. During training, the model is fed with the ground-truth tokens from the target language as inputs to the decoder, instead of using the model's own predictions. This approach ensures more stable and efficient training. However, it can lead to a discrepancy between training and inference, where the model struggles to handle its own generated text. To address this issue, scheduled sampling techniques and reinforcement learning methods have been explored.

A. Attention Mechanism in Sequence-to-Sequence Models:

One of the critical advancements in Seq2Seq models is the introduction of attention mechanisms. Attention mechanisms allow the model to focus on different parts of the input sequence during the decoding process. This enables the model to handle long-range dependencies and improve translation quality by aligning the source and target sequences more effectively.

A. Applications of Sequence-to-Sequence Models in Language Translation:

Seq2Seq models have found extensive applications in language translation tasks, with significant impact in various domains:

a) Neural Machine Translation (NMT): Seq2Seq models, particularly with attention mechanisms, have become the foundation of Neural Machine Translation systems, outperforming traditional statistical machine translation approaches.

b) Multilingual Translation: Seq2Seq models can be trained to translate between multiple language pairs, making them versatile for multilingual translation tasks.

c) Conversational AI: Seq2Seq models are employed in conversational agents and chatbots, enabling them to translate user inputs in different languages and respond in the user's preferred language.

d) Speech Translation: Seq2Seq models are adapted for speech-to-text translation, where the input is an audio speech signal, and the output is the corresponding text translation.

A. Challenges and Considerations:

While Seq2Seq models have shown remarkable success in language translation, several challenges and considerations need to be addressed:

a) Out-of-Vocabulary (OOV) Words: Seq2Seq models may struggle with out-of-vocabulary words that were not seen during training. Techniques like subword tokenization and handling unknown words are necessary to handle OOV words.

b) Rare Word Translation: Rare words or phrases with limited occurrences in the training data pose a challenge for Seq2Seq models. Leveraging techniques like copy mechanisms and translation lexicons can improve rare word translation.

c) Post-Editing and Evaluation: ***Post-editing of*** the generated translations is often required to ensure fluency and correctness. Evaluation metrics, such as BLEU and METEOR, are commonly used to assess the quality of machine-generated translations.

A. Advancements and Future Directions:

Seq2Seq models continue to evolve with ongoing research and advancements in NLP. Some exciting future directions include:

a) Transformer-based Seq2Seq Models: Transformers, a type of attention-based model, have gained popularity for their parallelization capabilities and superior performance in language tasks. Transformer-based Seq2Seq models are a promising direction for further improving translation quality.

b) Multimodal Translation: Integrating Seq2Seq models with other modalities, such as images or speech, opens up new possibilities for multimodal translation applications.

c) Low-Resource Translation: Research focuses on improving the performance of Seq2Seq models in low-resource settings, where there is limited training data for certain language pairs.

Sequence-to-Sequence models have become a fundamental technique in the field of language translation, enabling automatic translation between different languages. Their encoder-decoder architecture, along with attention mechanisms, has significantly improved translation quality and performance. Seq2Seq models find extensive applications in Neural Machine Translation, multilingual translation, conversational AI, and speech translation. However, addressing challenges related to rare words, out-of-vocabulary terms, and evaluation metrics remains essential for further advancements. As researchers continue to innovate and explore new approaches, Seq2Seq models are expected to remain at the forefront of language translation, facilitating seamless communication in a multilingual world.

Chapter 20: Natural Language Processing (NLP) with Machine Learning

1. Text Preprocessing and Tokenization

In the realm of natural language processing (NLP) and advanced machine learning techniques, text preprocessing and tokenization play pivotal roles in transforming raw textual data into a format suitable for further analysis and modeling. Text data, being unstructured and diverse in nature, requires careful handling to extract meaningful information and patterns. This process is crucial for various NLP tasks, such as sentiment analysis, machine translation, question-answering systems, and more.

- ***Introduction to Text Preprocessing:***

Text preprocessing is the initial step in NLP workflows, where textual data is cleaned and transformed into a structured format. The primary goal is to eliminate noise and irrelevant information that might hinder downstream analysis. The typical preprocessing steps involve converting text to lowercase, removing punctuation marks, and handling contractions. Additionally, techniques like stop word removal, stemming, and lemmatization are employed to further refine the data.

- ***Lowercasing and Removing Punctuation:***

One of the essential steps in text preprocessing is converting the entire text to lowercase. This step ensures that words with different letter cases are treated as the same, reducing the vocabulary size and simplifying subsequent analyses. Removing punctuation marks is equally crucial, as they often carry no significant meaning in most NLP tasks and can lead to unnecessary noise.

- ***Handling Contractions:***

Contractions like "don't," "can't," or "isn't" present a challenge for text analysis. Splitting contractions into their original forms (e.g., "do not," "cannot," "is not") allows the model to process these words correctly and comprehend their meanings.

- ***Stop Word Removal:***

Stop words are commonly occurring words in a language, such as "the," "and," "a," or "in." These words are often devoid of semantic meaning and contribute little to the overall context. Removing stop words reduces the dimensionality of the data and enhances the efficiency of subsequent algorithms.

- ***Stemming and Lemmatization:***

Stemming and lemmatization are techniques to reduce words to their base or root form, enabling words with the same root to be treated as identical tokens. Stemming is a faster, rule-based process that chops off suffixes, while lemmatization utilizes a vocabulary and morphological analysis to transform words into their base form. While stemming can sometimes produce non-dictionary words, lemmatization ensures valid dictionary words are generated.

- ***Tokenization:***

Tokenization is the process of breaking down a piece of text into individual units called tokens. These tokens can be words, characters, or subwords, depending on the chosen granularity. Word tokenization, the most common type, segments the text into words using whitespace or punctuation as delimiters. On the other hand, character tokenization treats each character as a separate token. More recently, subword tokenization, like Byte Pair Encoding (BPE) and SentencePiece, has gained popularity, especially in neural network-based models, to handle out-of-vocabulary words and create more compact vocabularies.

- ***Byte Pair Encoding (BPE):***

Byte Pair Encoding is an effective subword tokenization technique that recursively merges the most frequent character pairs to create subword tokens. This method dynamically adapts to the corpus vocabulary and can handle rare or unseen words by breaking them down into meaningful subword units. BPE has been instrumental in improving the performance of various language models, including transformer-based architectures like GPT.

- ***SentencePiece:***

SentencePiece is another subword tokenization approach that uses a unigram language model to segment text into variable-length subword units. It tokenizes sentences into a predefined vocabulary while effectively handling languages with complex word structures and characters. SentencePiece is particularly useful for languages with no explicit word delimiters and enables better representation for morphologically rich languages.

- ***Contextualized Token Embeddings:***

In advanced NLP models, such as ELMo, GPT, and BERT, contextualized token embeddings have revolutionized text representation. Unlike traditional word embeddings like Word2Vec and GloVe, which generate static representations, contextualized embeddings capture the meaning of a word based on its surrounding context within a sentence. This context-awareness significantly improves the model's understanding of nuances and word sense disambiguation.

In conclusion, text preprocessing and tokenization are critical components of advanced machine learning techniques in natural language processing. They lay the foundation for successful NLP tasks by converting raw text into a structured, meaningful format. Through techniques like lowercasing, removing punctuation, and handling contractions, the noise in the data is reduced. Additionally, stop word removal, stemming, and lemmatization help streamline the vocabulary and improve the model's efficiency. Subword tokenization techniques like Byte Pair Encoding and SentencePiece offer better handling of out-of-vocabulary words and complex languages. Furthermore, the advent of contextualized token embeddings has significantly enhanced the performance of NLP models, enabling them to grasp the subtle nuances of language. As NLP continues to advance, the importance of text preprocessing and tokenization remains paramount in extracting meaningful insights from vast volumes of textual data.

1. Word Embeddings: Word2Vec and GloVe

Word embeddings are essential representations of words in a vector space that capture semantic relationships between words. They are widely used in natural language processing (NLP) tasks and play a crucial role in advanced machine learning techniques. Two popular word embedding techniques are Word2Vec and GloVe, which offer distinct approaches to generate meaningful word representations.

- ***Introduction to Word Embeddings***

Word embeddings address the challenge of representing words in a format that machines can understand and process effectively. In traditional NLP models, words are encoded as one-hot vectors, where each word is represented by a binary vector with a single '1' corresponding to the word's position in the vocabulary and '0's elsewhere. However, one-hot encoding lacks semantic information and fails to capture relationships between words. This limitation motivated the development of word embeddings.

Word embeddings represent words as dense, low-dimensional vectors in continuous vector spaces. The key idea behind word embeddings is to place similar words closer together in the vector space, making it possible for machine learning models to understand the contextual meaning of words. By leveraging word embeddings, NLP tasks like sentiment analysis, machine translation, and text generation have witnessed significant improvements.

- ***Word2Vec - Distributed Representations***

Word2Vec, proposed by Mikolov et al., is one of the pioneering techniques for generating word embeddings. It operates on the assumption that words appearing in similar contexts share semantic similarities. There are two main architectures for Word2Vec: Continuous Bag of Words (CBOW) and Skip-gram.

In CBOW, the model predicts the target word based on its context words. For example, given the sentence "The cat sat on the mat," the CBOW model tries to predict "sat" using the context words "The," "cat," "on," and "the." On the other hand, Skip-gram predicts context words based on the target word. Both CBOW and Skip-gram models are trained on a large corpus of text data using stochastic gradient descent or hierarchical softmax.

Word2Vec's distributed representations enable the model to capture word similarities and analogies. For instance, in the vector space, words like "king" and "queen" are positioned close to each other, and the vector representing "king - man + woman" is approximately equal to the vector representing "queen." These properties demonstrate the semantic relationships that Word2Vec can learn from the data.

- ***GloVe - Global Vectors for Word Representation***

GloVe (Global Vectors for Word Representation), developed by Pennington et al., is another significant word embedding technique that considers global word co-occurrence statistics. Unlike Word2Vec, which is based on local context windows, GloVe takes a global approach, considering the frequency of word pairs co-occurring in the entire corpus.

The underlying principle of GloVe is that word pairs with higher co-occurrence frequencies are more likely to have stronger semantic relationships. It constructs a word-to-word co-occurrence matrix, where each element represents the number of times two words appear together within a certain context window. GloVe then factorizes this matrix to obtain word embeddings, aiming to preserve the ratios of co-occurrence probabilities between words.

GloVe's global perspective offers a unique advantage in capturing semantic relationships across the entire corpus. It can handle rare words better than Word2Vec because it does not rely solely on local context windows. Moreover, GloVe embeddings exhibit a linear structure, enabling meaningful algebraic operations like analogies, similar to Word2Vec.

- ***Application and Evaluation of Word Embeddings***

Both Word2Vec and GloVe embeddings have demonstrated remarkable performance across a range of NLP tasks. Sentiment analysis, for example, benefits from the rich semantic information captured in the embeddings, allowing models to understand the nuances in word meanings and their impact on the overall sentiment of a sentence.

Machine translation also benefits significantly from word embeddings. In neural machine translation models, word embeddings are used to represent the source and target languages, facilitating the conversion of text between different languages more effectively.

To evaluate the quality of word embeddings, researchers often use intrinsic and extrinsic evaluation methods. Intrinsic evaluation assesses the embeddings directly through tasks like word similarity and analogy tests. Extrinsic evaluation involves integrating the embeddings into downstream NLP tasks and measuring the improvement in performance compared to other embedding techniques or traditional methods.

- ***Advancements and Future Directions***

Since the introduction of Word2Vec and GloVe, word embedding techniques have evolved significantly. Researchers have explored more sophisticated architectures, such as ELMo (Embeddings from Language Models) and BERT (Bidirectional Encoder Representations from Transformers), which leverage deep neural networks to generate contextualized word embeddings.

Contextualized embeddings take into account the surrounding words in a sentence, allowing them to capture word meaning variations based on the sentence context. This advancement has led to substantial improvements in various NLP tasks, including sentiment analysis, question answering, and named entity recognition.

Looking ahead, word embeddings will likely continue to play a central role in NLP and advanced machine learning techniques. As language models become larger and more complex, the development of innovative word embedding methods will remain crucial to improve the understanding of language and drive the progress of artificial intelligence applications that rely on natural language understanding.

1. Sentiment Analysis and Text Classification with NLP

Sentiment Analysis and Text Classification are essential natural language processing (NLP) tasks that involve the use of advanced machine learning techniques to understand and categorize the sentiment or meaning of text data. These tasks have significant applications across various industries, including social media monitoring, customer feedback analysis, and market research.

- ***Introduction to Sentiment Analysis and Text Classification***

Sentiment Analysis, also known as opinion mining, aims to determine the sentiment expressed in a piece of text, such as positive, negative, or neutral. This process involves analyzing the words, phrases, and context to infer the writer's emotions or attitudes towards a particular subject or topic. On the other hand, Text Classification involves categorizing text data into predefined classes or categories. For example, classifying emails as spam or not spam, identifying the topic of news articles, or classifying customer reviews into sentiment categories (e.g., positive, negative, neutral).

Both Sentiment Analysis and Text Classification are challenging tasks due to the inherent complexity of human language. Language is ambiguous and context-dependent, making it difficult for traditional rule-based systems to achieve high accuracy. Advanced machine learning techniques, especially those based on deep learning, have revolutionized these tasks by enabling models to learn intricate patterns and representations from vast amounts of data.

- ***Data Preparation and Preprocessing***

Data preparation is a crucial step in sentiment analysis and text classification. The quality and size of the training dataset significantly impact the model's performance. The dataset should be well-annotated, with clear labels for sentiment categories or classes. It should also be diverse, covering various topics and different writing styles to ensure generalization to unseen data.

Preprocessing the text data is equally important to remove noise and irrelevant information. Common preprocessing steps include lowercasing all text, removing special characters and punctuation, tokenizing text into individual words or subwords, and removing stop words (commonly used words like "the," "is," etc.). Additionally, techniques like stemming or lemmatization can be applied to reduce words to their root forms, which helps in reducing the dimensionality of the data and improving model efficiency.

- ***Feature Extraction and Word Embeddings***

In traditional machine learning methods, text data is often represented as a high-dimensional vector, where each feature corresponds to a specific word or n-gram (sequence of n words). However, this approach suffers from the curse of dimensionality and may not capture semantic relationships between words effectively.

To address this, word embeddings (e.g., Word2Vec, GloVe) are widely used to represent words in dense, low-dimensional vector spaces. These embeddings capture semantic information and word similarities, which is crucial for sentiment analysis and text classification. By utilizing pre-trained word embeddings, models can leverage large corpora of text to improve performance, especially when the labeled dataset is limited.

- ***Traditional Machine Learning Models for Text Classification***

Before the advent of deep learning, traditional machine learning models like Naive Bayes, Support Vector Machines (SVM), and Random Forests were commonly used for text classification. These models rely on handcrafted features and shallow learning techniques.

Naive Bayes is a probabilistic classifier that assumes conditional independence between features, making it computationally efficient and effective for text classification tasks with relatively small datasets. SVM, on the other hand, aims to find a hyperplane that best separates data points into different classes, providing a powerful tool for binary and multi-class text classification. Random Forests, an ensemble method, combine multiple decision trees to make predictions, offering robustness and accuracy.

- ***Deep Learning Models for Sentiment Analysis and Text Classification***

The rise of deep learning has led to significant advancements in sentiment analysis and text classification. Convolutional Neural Networks (CNNs) and Recurrent Neural Networks (RNNs) have shown exceptional performance in handling text data due to their ability to learn hierarchical features and capture contextual information.

CNNs are well-suited for tasks involving local patterns, such as identifying sentiment-bearing phrases or expressions within longer sentences. They use convolutional layers to extract relevant features from the text and max-pooling layers to reduce dimensionality and preserve important information.

RNNs, on the other hand, are designed to handle sequential data and capture dependencies across time steps. Long Short-Term Memory (LSTM) and Gated Recurrent Unit (GRU) are popular variants of RNNs that address the vanishing gradient problem, enabling them to model longer sequences effectively.

Moreover, the advent of transformer-based architectures, such as BERT (Bidirectional Encoder Representations from Transformers), has revolutionized text classification. BERT utilizes self-attention mechanisms to capture contextual information bidirectionally, achieving state-of-the-art results in various NLP tasks, including sentiment analysis and text classification.

- ***Evaluation and Challenges***

Evaluating the performance of sentiment analysis and text classification models is crucial to ensure their effectiveness. Common evaluation metrics include accuracy, precision, recall, F1-score, and area under the Receiver Operating Characteristic (ROC) curve.

However, sentiment analysis can be particularly challenging due to the subjectivity of human emotions and the presence of sarcasm and irony in text. Additionally, domain-specific language and linguistic variations pose difficulties in achieving high accuracy across different domains.

Furthermore, the availability of labeled data is a significant challenge for supervised learning approaches. Labeling large amounts of text data manually can be time-consuming and expensive. Semi-supervised and unsupervised learning methods, along with transfer learning techniques, are explored to overcome these limitations and improve model performance with limited labeled data.

- ***Future Directions and Conclusion***

As the field of NLP continues to advance, sentiment analysis and text classification will remain at the forefront of research and development. Future directions may involve exploring more sophisticated transformer-based models, leveraging multi-modal data (combining text with images, audio, etc.), and enhancing the interpretability of models to gain better insights into their decision-making processes.

Overall, sentiment analysis and text classification are vital tools for understanding human sentiment and classifying text data into meaningful categories.

The integration of advanced machine learning techniques and the continuous improvement of NLP models will continue to drive progress in these areas, enabling a wide range of applications across industries and domains.

Data Science Fusion: Integrating Maths, Python, and Machine Learning

Written by Nibedita Sahu.

Nibedita Sahu is a dynamic Data Science enthusiast, Python programmer, and versatile writer. Armed with a bachelor's degree in Mathematics, she has a passion for exploring the limitless possibilities of data analysis and machine learning. Nibedita's flair for writing extends beyond data science as she is a skilled technology article writer and tech blogger. With a knack for breaking down complex concepts into digestible pieces, she empowers readers to embrace the fascinating world of data science. Her passion for technology drives her to share her knowledge with the world, making her a compelling and accomplished author.

www.ingramcontent.com/pod-product-compliance
Lightning Source LLC
LaVergne TN
LVHW100246210926
848480LV00003B/839
9798233791345